Python Programming for Beginners

The Complete Guide to Mastering Python in 7 Days with Hands-On Exercises –Top Secret Coding Tips to Get an Unfair Advantage and Land Your Dream Job!

Philip Robbins

Table of Contents

As a thank you for your trust in my book, you will have access to **an exclusive gift** at the end of this book: **a long list of Python interview questions and answers** (for beginners and advanced).

I personally feel that learning Python can be extremely helpful if you really want to make that career switch and find your dream job. Since coding can be done from anywhere, you could even find a remote opportunity, giving you a healthy work-life balance where you have more time for yourself or your family

Learning this innovative programming language has already helped so many people, and I hope that it will help you too!

Philip

Introduction

Computers can be categorized as machines with no inherent intelligence, but they have drastically helped to advance our world in countless ways. With computers, our world runs much more efficiently and error-free—we tell them what to do, and they deliver flawless results. Computer programmers are the people who communicate with computers in what are called programming languages, and they have been doing so for many years. These programming languages vary based on their working systems, just as human language varies based on region.

One of these computer programming languages is called Python, and in the computer realm, this is a quite popular (and easy to learn) high-level programming language. This book will teach you Python in an intuitive way. Even if you have no experience with any programming language, you will be able to grasp the basics of Python and put them to use.

What Is Python?

Python is a high-level programming language that is popular within the programming community. It is simple, versatile, and contains an extensive library of third-party frameworks. It is also considered to be one of the most popular modern programming languages, being highly accessible for beginners. You can even use it to create software in your programming domain of choice.

Accredited universities such as Stanford teach Python to computer science graduates as an introductory language. Many online courses that explore programming basics also use Python as the default language. As you can see, it's very prevalent and therefore highly useful to learn. For these reasons, I am happy that you have chosen this book to help you learn Python quickly and intuitively.

Who Am I?

If you search the Internet, you are likely to find thousands of resources available for learning Python. And while this is great, it can also be overwhelming—therefore, many beginners can get frustrated because they do not have concise instructions with a clear walkthrough.

My name is Philip Robbins, and I am determined to offer a clear pathway for beginners to excel. I have more than twenty years of experience working in the field of software development using Python, and I am an expert Python programmer. My love for programming started a decade ago, when I avidly played video games. It all started with my enthusiasm to mod a Pokémon game that I was playing. My will to successfully change a small bit of code to feel accomplished sparked excitement to understand programming logic and variables at a young age. With some modding experience, I was able to understand how programs work and spent time experimenting with different programming languages.

Fast forward a few years, and I started creating small scripts that could automate workflow. However, I had still not chosen a particular programming language, and this made it challenging to be an actual software program developer. All of the programming languages I had tried, such as C and Pearl, were challenging to implement and almost made me quit programming due to massive frustration many times. Fortunately, during those turbulent times

I discovered Python in its initial stages. Python first began as a hobby project by one developer, so its initial form was not very clean. Once it gained in popularity, however, fellow developers began to notice the open-source project. This spurred them to add their own contributions as well. Thus, they effectively modeled it into the efficient programming language it is today.

Within a few months of learning Python basics, I began implementing my own pre-existing code into Python. I was astounded by the code's portability as well as its lack of clutter. Once I learned how Python worked, there was no turning back. I began writing my software and publishing them using different stores. Even though my main job was to create web applications, I successfully created several other side projects in various domains with the help of Python.

Now that I am proficient in Python, I am interested in helping people who are struggling to learn this coding language. Even when I was first modding games in the beginning stages, I always had a passion for quickly assisting people in learning programming. I use layman's terms to explain complex topics, and this has helped many of my friends and colleagues understand them better. My passion for programming and teaching has compelled me to write this book in order to help beginners who are new to Python.

How Can This Book Help You?

Though Python programming looks easy to implement, in truth it is not. If you have a thorough understanding of the several foundational topics Python contains and how you can utilize them to solve problems, this is incredibly helpful. As such, this book provides you with the theoretical knowledge you need to know in order to understand the foundations and practicality of the programming language you are trying to use.

To get the most out of this book, we recommend cognitive learning techniques. These will enhance your experience with this material.

- Use cognitive memory techniques such as Memory Palace to keenly remember the data. However, there is a difference between simply mugging up the required information in your brain versus formally storing it when using f cognitive techniques.

- Use mind maps to map different concepts in order to quickly implement them in your projects. Mind maps are cognitive learning tools that use visual excellence via a short diagram to remember large amounts of data easily.
- Use the passive recall technique to quickly review all of the topics you have learned in this book. Passive recall can also help strengthen your programming foundations.
- Don't just use the code given in this book. Instead, reimplement your code using similar strategies. Using the simple copy-and-paste technique will not help you in creating your code.
- Use the Feynman technique to explain all of the basic programming concepts you have learned in this book to someone unaware of the subject. You have a strong knowledge of the core foundations if you can explain concepts in simple terms.

As a programming language, Python expects you to be as innovative as possible. Therefore, if you treat programming with Python like solving a puzzle, then you will intuitively discover ways to trick your brain into creating complex code logic for addressing real-world problems. This book helps you to become as effective as possible with Python programming.

How Can You Help This Book?

Writing this book has not been easy—in fact, spending hours debugging is easier than writing a book. I'll be honest with you, for the first time in my life, I have experienced writer's block. Knowing the topics is one thing, but attempting to explain them in a logical, concise, synthetic, and organized way is quite another.

Also, since I have preferred to avoid the services of any publishing house, I can call myself an "independent author." This is a personal choice. It has not been easy, but my obsession with helping others has prevailed.

This is why it would give me immense pleasure if you could leave a positive review on Amazon. That would mean so much to me and would greatly help spreading this material to others. I would suggest the following:

1. **If you haven't already done, scan the QR code at the end of the book** and download the pdf with the Python interview Q&As and the solutions to the exercises. Going through the book with that list is much more fun!

2. **Scan the QR code below and <u>leave a quick review on Amazon</u>!**

The best way to do it? <u>Upload a brief video</u> with you talking about what you think about the book!

If this is too much for you, that's not a problem at all! A review with a couple of pictures of the book would still be very nice of you!

NOTE: You don't have to feel obliged, but it would be highly appreciated!
I'm excited to start this journey with you. Are you ready to dive in?
Then let's move on.
Happy reading!

Chapter 1: Introduction to Python

Python is a powerful programming language that is easy to learn, has a strong foundation, and can support multiparadigm workflows. As a result, it is an excellent starting point for beginners who want to delve into programming. Python's popularity stems primarily from its lack of clutter and boilerplate code.

For example, writing a simple snake game in C or C++ usually requires 300 lines of code. In contrast, with Python you can limit the number of lines of code to less than 200. This significant difference in terms of implementation contributed to Python becoming the most popular open-source language in the world. Python quickly became the waypoint for the open-source revolution, with so many enthusiastic programmers and developers writing thousands of libraries for various computer fields.

History of Python

Guido van Rossum, who created Python, made it as a side project over the Christmas break. Using what he learned working with the ABC programming language, he made an interpreted programming language that is easy to understand and use. He first used Python to impress hackers in an online community with his knowledge of how Unix works.

But after getting feedback from his fellow programmers, he worked on it for a few months to make it better. So, he made a programming language that was easy and quick to understand. Guido van Rossum has been called the "benevolent dictator" of the Python community because of what he has done for the Python project. Open-source developers can be given this high award.

Python has always been one of the 10 most popular programming languages, according to TIOBE rankings, ever since it came out. Python's simple way of solving problems has helped it beat other programming languages, like Pearl, and become one of the easier ones for beginners to learn.

Python is based on the idea that there is only one way to solve a problem, which is different from the idea behind programming languages like Pearl, which is that there are many ways to solve a problem. So, Python gave the programming community the discipline it needed and made software development grow by a factor of ten.

Look at the Python Applications below to see how important Python was to programmers around the world.

Applications of Python

Python made its mark in many areas of science and technology today.

1. Web Domain

Python has had most of its early effect as a programming language on web technology. While Java was the most popular thing on the web, Python wasn't as popular. Over time, Python has become popular among web developers thanks to third-party frameworks like Django and Tornado.

In the twenty years since then, Python has become one of the most popular scripting languages for websites, second only to JavaScript. Python is a programming language that is used by big companies like Google, Facebook, and Netflix. A well-known web framework called Django can also help programmers write backend code for a number of APIs.

Python is also popular for automating tasks, so it is often used to make bots like Pinflux.

2. Scientific Computing

Python is popular with scientists because it is free for anyone to use. Also, programs like Numpy and Scipy make it easier for computer scientists to do experiments with less code. Since Python is also better at mathematical calculations and software, Scientists have no choice but to use it these days.

3. Machine Learning and AI

AI and machine learning are now two technologies that can be used together to give more jobs to developers. There are a lot of third-party libraries for Python, like Tensorflow, that are all about implementing Machine Learning algorithms.

Python is also very good at adapting to technologies like Deep Learning and Natural Language Processing. This makes it one of the main candidates to become a better language for making AI-related technology.

4. Linux and the Management of Databases

As businesses around the world grow, there is a big need for developers who can manage databases and internal systems well. Develop engineers need to know enough about different operating systems, like Linux, and they also need to know enough about Python to automate other procedures that are needed to test how well methods work on an internal network.

5. Penetration Testing and Hacking

Python is also used by hackers with both good and bad intentions. For example, white-hat hackers use Python tools that are widely used to do penetration testing. On the other hand, hackers with bad intentions use Python scripting to make exploits that automatically steal sensitive information from their targets.

Python's ability to be used in almost any area of computer programming has led to the development of several other high-level programming languages, like Go, Groovy, and Swift. Python spread the idea that programming should be as simple as possible.

Different Versions of Python

When Python came out at the start of the 1990s, it wasn't as good as it is now. Rossum built the library without any help from anyone else, so it had a lot of bugs and mistakes. But because Python was so popular right away in the programming community, hundreds of independent developers helped Rossum make a much bigger project in the two years after the first version came out.

Python was also able to get a lot of smart people to check and change the code because it was open source. Because of this, the Python core programming team has put out two main versions, Python 2 and Python 3, for developers all over the world in the last 20 years.

In 2022, Python 2 is still used by a lot of programmers, even though Python core developers no longer support it. Choosing which version to use depends on what you are doing.

Python 2

Python 2 is now an old version that came out in the year 2000. Still, it has been the most used version of Python for more than 20 years. Python 2 is easier to use and has a lot more frameworks and libraries from outside sources that can be used for development.

Even though Python 2.7 will no longer get official updates after 2021, it is still the best version for many software domains. But it's hard to move all of the frameworks and libraries from Python 2 to Python 3, so many companies still use Python 2 as their default version.

Python 3

Python 3.9 is the most recent version of the programming language that developers can use. Python 3 is faster and gives developers many more classes for working with the core library. Compared to Python 2, it is also easy to keep up with.

Which one Should I Choose?

Which version of Python you use should depend on what kind of software you are making. For example, a lot of data scientists use Python 3, while developers who work with legacy software use Python 2 to connect components.

Note:

All of the Python code in this book is written in Python 3, since it makes more sense for beginners to start with a newer version.

Why You Should Learn Python

Python started to become more popular in the early 1990s, when companies all over the world started to use the internet's power to make complex web applications. Traditional programming languages like C and C+ were hard to learn and made it hard for programmers to write good code quickly. During this time, Python helped a number of companies make libraries that worked well with the C and C++ libraries they already had. Also, programmers started using Python to quickly deploy code because it was easier to work with than other high-level languages.

By learning about some of Python's many benefits, you can see how powerful and easy it can be for developers with different backgrounds in computer science.

It Is an Interpreted Language

Instead of using a compiler to run instructions like other programming languages do, Python uses a new piece of software called an interpreter. Instead of taking a lot of time to run a program with a compiler, the interpreter uses modern computer techniques to parse the code before the program is run. This dynamic parse time can cut down on the time you have to wait while the program is running. Python also uses parts of natural language to get rid of unproductive ways of coding that can slow down production. Because of how it is set up, it is also easy to automate programming in Python, which is why system developers and Linux administrators like it so much.

It is Open Source

One of the first things that led to the open-source revolution was Python. Because Python is open source, you can change any code and share it on your own. Open-source culture also makes it easier for programmers all over the world to share their knowledge and resources to make libraries and frameworks that can help developers make new projects.

As a beginner, having one-click access to both complex and simple projects can help you understand how programming works and make it easy to make new, creative projects.

It Supports Multiple Paradigms

To write and run code, different programming languages use different programming paradigms. Java, on the other hand, uses an object-oriented paradigm, while C uses a functional paradigm. A programming paradigm changes how developers work and how they try to solve a problem.

Python supports multiple paradigms, like the structured, functional, and object-oriented paradigms. This makes it a good choice for programmers who want to solve problems in different ways.

It Uses a Garbage Collection Mechanism

Managing memory is an important skill for application developers to have. High-level languages such as Java and C use complex data management techniques. Even though these mechanisms work perfectly, it takes a lot of time to keep them in good shape. In Python, on the other hand, memory is handled by garbage collectors. You can easily use the data and variables that this strategy no longer uses.

It Is Easy to Understand

One of the many reasons developers like Python is that it is easy to read. All of the code is easy to understand, which makes it easy to keep up. When Python code is easier to read, its quality goes up, and when the quality goes up, it takes less time to fix bugs in the code.

Portability

Python can also run on any operating system, which makes it easy for developers to use it in different ways with just a few hours of work. Users only need to install the interpreter on their system for Python programs to work.

For instance, let's say a programmer writes a program for Linux that makes it easy to automate SQL database management. Then, anyone who has access to the code can place it on Windows or Mac machines by changing a few parts of it.

It Has Great Custom Libraries

If you want a programming language to be widely used, it needs to have great libraries. Developers can play around with a lot of these libraries in Python.

Aside from these custom libraries, programmers can also make interesting software with the standard libraries that the Python core development team gives them.

It Supports Component Integration

Python makes it easy for programmers to add new code to code that has already been written. Also, its advanced integration of components makes it a good choice for making advanced customization options for different software applications.

Component integration keeps developers busy by adding new features to older software so it can run on newer operating systems.

It Has a Great Community

The Python community is very helpful and can help new programmers quickly solve any problems they run into while writing code. Aside from Python forums, resources and well-written guides from a variety of experienced programmers can help developers get past any problems.

Since there are a lot of open-source Python projects on GitHub, a hobbyist programmer can just look at the code to see how complex logic is implemented in software.

How to Install Python

To write Python code, you must install an interpreter on your system. Without this interpreter, no developer would be able to write or run Python programs. Python can be put on any modern operating system because it can be moved around. In this section, we'll talk about how to install Python on Linux, Mac, and Windows.

How do I Install Python in Linux?

Since most programmers use Linux as their main operating system, we'll start by installing Python on your local machine using Linux. Linux is a free operating system that most programmers and businesses use. Because of this, Python is already on many Linux distributions.

To see if Python is installed on your Linux system, use the CTRL+ALT+N command to open a new command terminal.

When the new command terminal opens, type the following command into it.

Terminal Code:

```
$ Python3
```

If Python is installed on your system, the license information for the version of Python that is installed will show up in your terminal.

If you get the output "command not found," on the other hand, it means that Python is not installed on your system. Since Python is not installed, you can now use the package managers for Linux to install Python for different distros.

Before installing any software on Linux, you must first update all the tools on Linux and make sure there are no conflict errors that could stop Python installation.

Terminal Code:

```
$ sudo apt-get upgrade
```

You can use the code above to update package files on a Linux system that is based on Debian.

Use the following Pacman command to upgrade packages on an Arch-based system.

Terminal Code:

```
$ sudo pacman -S
```

After upgrading the packages, you can use the commands below to install Python on your Linux system.

Terminal code for Debian systems:

```
$ sudo apt-get install Python3
```

Terminal code for Arch systems:

```
$ pacman -u Python3
```

Look at the official Python documentation to install in other Linux distributions like Gentoo and kali.

How do I Install Python on macOS?

macOS is the operating system that Apple makes by default. Python 2 is often installed as native software because it is built with UNIX support.

Make sure you open a new terminal from Settings > Utilities > Terminal to see if macOS is installed on your Apple-supported hardware.

Enter the following command once a new terminal has been opened.

Terminal Code:

```
$ python3
```

If you don't see a Python version message, it means that Python is not installed on your system. To install Python from scratch, use homebrew.

Terminal Code:

```
$ brew install Python3
```

How do I Install Python on Windows?

Windows is the most used operating system in the world, based on the number of people who use it. Many people and programmers use Windows because it is easy to use, and there are many ways for Python programmers to quickly get their code into Windows.

To install Python on your Windows system, you must first download an executable package from the official Python website. Once the package is downloaded, you can install the software by double-clicking on it. For Python code development to work on some Windows systems, you may need to change the environment variables in the Control panel.

Once everything is set up as needed, open a command prompt window to see if the Python interpreter is correctly installed.

Command Prompt Code:

```
>> Python —version
```

If the command tells you what version of Python is installed, then Python is set up correctly on your system. If not, you might have to copy and paste the error into Google or use Python forums to figure out what's wrong.

Chapter 2: PyCharm and IDLE

Once you've installed Python, you'll need a development environment on your system to write programs. Even though you can work with the basic IDLE that comes with a basic Python installation, developers are encouraged to use IDEs like PyCharm for better software development workflow. IDEs make developers more productive and make it easier for them to find bugs in code that has already been turned into software.

Why Is Python Interpreter Good?

The Python interpreter is great because it is flexible and has more features than traditional compilers. For example, compared to compilers, a Python interpreter makes you wait less. Compilers run the code after it has been written and checked for mistakes. The interpreter, on the other hand, checks the code as it is being written and lets the programmer know if there is a problem before the code is run. Real-time error reporting is a good way for beginners to learn how to code while they are doing it.

When you install Python on your computer, it also installs IDLE, which stands for "Integrated development and learning environment." To start IDLE, you can type "Python" into your favorite terminal interface. The REPL mechanism is used by IDLE to show output on the computer screen. REPL is a basic method that Python interpreters use to check the lines that have been written and parse them so that they can be shown on the screen. This is done based on the input and output that are given.

Python IDLE can be a great tool for people who are just starting to learn how to code. Even though most enterprise software development is done on integrated development environments (IDEs) like PyCharm, learning some basic commands for Python IDLE can help you understand how Python interpretation works.

How to Use the Python IDLE Shell?

Once Python is installed, open a terminal or command prompt and type the following command to start the IDLE.

Command:

```
$ python
```

As shown below, when you press Enter or Return, a new shell will open.

```
>>>
```

You can test how Python IDLE works on your system by using some of the basic math or Print commands.

Program Code:

```
>>> print ("This is a sample to check that the IDLE works")
```

Output:

```
This is a sample to check that the IDLE works
```

When the Enter button is pressed, the program goes into REPL mode, and the text between the double quotes is shown on the computer screen. This is because IDLE knew that the shell window used the print() method to show strings.

You can also use math operations to test the IDLE workflow.

Program Code:

```
>>> 8 + 3
```

Output:

```
11
```

Exercise:

Use the IDLE window to check the results of other math operations, like multiplication and division.

Note:

It's important to remember that as soon as you close the terminal window, all of your code will be lost. So, even if we use an IDLE, we need to make sure that all of our code is put into a Python file.

How to Use IDLE to Open Python Files?

IDLE makes it simple to open and read Python files with a .py extension on the terminal. Keep in mind that this command will only function if you are in the same directory as the Python file.

Program Code:

```
$ python mysample.py
```

The prior command will open the previously written code for the programmers to read.

- IDLE can automatically highlight unique syntax components.
- IDLE assists developers in completing code by providing hints.
- IDLE has the ability to easily indent code.

To use any Python files on your IDLE shell, use the GUI file option and click the 'Open' button. However, advanced programmers advise using the path to open Python files if you are not in the same directory.

How to Change These Files?

Once the files are open in IDLE, you can begin editing the code in the file with your keyboard. Because IDLE provides line numbers, developers can easily manipulate any non-indented code. Once the file has been edited, press the F5 key to run it on your terminal code.

If there are no errors, the output will be displayed; otherwise, the traceback errors will be displayed.

While not as efficient as other advanced IDEs on the market, Python IDLE serves as an excellent debugging tool. It has several debugging features, including the ability to place endpoints, catch exceptions, and parse code to quickly debug the code. However, it is not ideal and may cause issues if your Project library grows.

Regardless of how little it offers, IDLE is possibly the best developer tool for complete beginners.

Exercise:

Develop a new program in Python IDLE to add two numbers and debug it with breakpoints. If you are unfamiliar with any programming components, you are free to use any Internet resources to solve this simple problem.

IDE (Integrated Development Environment)

Python IDLE is frequently not recommended for real-world application development due to its inability to handle highly demanding projects. Developers are instead asked to manage and develop their code in specialized development environments known as IDEs. Furthermore, IDEs provide programmers with tight integration capabilities with various libraries.

IDE characteristics

1. Simple Integration Into Libraries & Frameworks

One of the important features of IDEs is that they make it simple to integrate libraries and frameworks into software applications. IDLE requires you to assign them individually each time you use them, whereas IDEs do the hard work for you by autocompleting various import statements. Many IDEs also support direct git repository integration.

2. Integration of Object Oriented Design

Many Python programmers who create applications employ an object-oriented paradigm. Unfortunately, Python IDLE does not include any tools to help developers create applications while adhering to object-oriented principles. All modern IDEs include components such as class hierarchy diagrams to help developers get their projects started with better programming logic.

3. Syntax Highlighting

Syntax highlighting assists programmers in increasing productivity and avoiding simple, obvious errors. For example, you cannot use reserved keywords like 'if' to name variables. The IDE automatically detects this error and assists developers in understanding it through syntax highlighting.

4. Code Completion

All modern IDEs use advanced artificial intelligence and machine learning techniques to complete code for developers automatically. The IDEs gather a lot of information from the packages you use, so they can suggest different variables or methods based on your input and the logic you're writing. Even though auto-completion is a useful feature, you should never rely entirely on it because it can occasionally disrupt program execution and cause errors.

5. Version Control

Version control is a major source of frustration for developers. For example, if you use private libraries and frameworks in your application, they may occasionally be updated, causing your application to fail. As a developer, you must be aware of these changes and implement new code execution for all applications to function properly. The version control mechanism enables developers to easily update their core application without causing any disruptions to previously written code. IDEs support direct version control with websites like GitHub.

IDEs can also provide advanced debugging features for developers in addition to these features. For example, the most popular Python IDEs for independent developers and organizations are PyCharm and Eclipse. We will use PyCharm as our default IDE in this book because it is much more efficient than Eclipse and much easier to set up.

PyCharm

PyCharm is a Python-only IDE produced by JetBrains, a pioneer in software tool development. Initially, the JetBrains team created PyCharm to manage their IDEs for other programming languages. However, due to its portability, the JetBrains team later released it as a standalone product for users worldwide. PyCharm is available for all major operating systems and comes in two flavors: community and professional.

1. The community version is open-source, free software that anyone can use to write Python code. It does, however, have some limitations, particularly in terms of version control and third-party library integration.
2. The professional version is a paid IDE that offers advanced functionality and numerous integration options to developers. For example, using the professional version of PyCharm IDE, developers can easily create web or data science applications.

What Features Does PyCharm Provide?

PyCharm is well-known for its unique features for enthusiastic Python developers, as well as its high-quality integration capabilities.

1. Code Editor

PyCharm's code editor is among the best in the industry. When working with new projects in this editor, you will be astounded by the code completion abilities. Furthermore, JetBrains has used several advanced machine learning models to make the IDE intelligent enough to understand even the most complex programming blocks and provide useful suggestions.

While working as a developer, the PyCharm editor can also be customized for a better viewing experience. Light and dark themes are available to users, allowing you to change the theme based on your mood.

2. Code Navigation

PyCharm's complex and comprehensive file organization system makes it simple for programmers to manage files. Bookmarks and lens mode, for example, can assist Python programmers in effectively managing their essential programming blocks and code logic.

3. Refactoring

PyCharm includes advanced refactoring features that allow developers to easily change the names of files, classes, and methods without breaking the program. When you use IDLE to refactor your code, it immediately breaks the code because the default Python IDLE is not intelligent enough to distinguish between new and old names.

When it comes to updating their code or migrating to a much better third-party library for one of their software components, most Python developers use Advanced refactoring capabilities.

4. Web Technology Integration

The majority of Python developers work in the web domain, which accounts for a sizable portion of the software industry. PyCharm simplifies the integration of developers' software with Python web frameworks such as Django. PyCharm is also intelligent enough to understand HTML, CSS, and JavaScript code, which are commonly used by web developers to create web services.

All of these features make it simple for Python web developers to integrate existing web code into a Python framework.

5. Integration With Scientific Libraries

PyCharm is also well-known for its strong support for scientific and advanced mathematical libraries like SciPy and NumPy. While it will never completely replace your data integration and cleaning setup, it will assist you in developing a basic pseudo logic for all of your data science projects.

6. Software Testing

PyCharm can execute high-level unit testing strategies for even the most complex and large projects with numerous members. It also includes advanced debugging tools and remote configuration capabilities for using the Alpha and beta testing workflows.

How to Use PyCharm?

With enough information about PyCharm, you should be convinced that it is a necessary development tool for your local system. This section contains the information you need to install PyCharm and understand how to use it to better manage your Python projects.

Step—1: Install PyCharm

PyCharm can be installed on almost any operating system. To begin, obtain the installation package from the official website or one of the numerous package managers.

Navigate to the JetBrains official website and click the downloads tab in the upper right corner. Now, depending on your operating system, download the executable or dmg file and double-click it to follow the instructions on the screen.

To download a professional version of the software, you must first provide payment information in order to download a trial version. When the trial period expires, you will be charged and will be able to use the professional version without issue.

Note:

In order for the PyCharm IDE to install successfully on your system, Python must be installed. This is because it detects the Python path and installs the software's core libraries automatically.

Step—2: Create New Projects

After installing the software, launch the PyCharm IDE from your applications or from the Desktop icon. When you open PyCharm, a new popup will appear, allowing you to start a new project from scratch. You can open a new project using the button in the upper left corner of the software interface using the "File" option. Other options include importing and exporting existing projects or quickly saving current working projects.

When you first open a Python project, you will be prompted to choose which Python interpreter you want to use for all programming procedures. If you don't know where to look for the Python interpreter, choose 'virtualenv,' which will automatically search the system and find one for you.

Step—3: Using PyCharm to Organize

Creating new folders and resources for your Program files is essential once you begin creating projects with PyCharm.

To create a new folder on your project interface, simply select the new --> folder option. You can include any Python scripts or assets used in your software in this section.

When you create a new file in a separate folder, a file with the.py extension is created. As a result, if you want to create different class files or templates, you must do so explicitly while creating a file in your folder.

Step—4: Advanced Features in PyCharm

Once the code is written and integrated, you can use the built-in IDLE interface or the PyCharm unique output interface to run it quickly.

All code you write will be automatically saved in real time, so you won't have to worry about losing any critical project data due to a bad network connection or power outage. To save a copy of a project on your local system, simply press Ctrl S or Cmd S.

When the program is finished, press Shift + F10 to run and compile the code with the help of an interpreter.

Using the Ctrl F or Cmd F commands, you can search for any method, variable, or snippet in your project. Simply use this shortcut and enter the information you're looking for.

Once the Python code has been imported and deployed to the required operating systems, you must begin setting up a debugging project environment in order to constantly clear bugs on your system. To place breakpoints and solve logical problems without messing up the entire code logic or breaking the core program, press Shift + F9.

Python Style Guide

Python programming grew in popularity among programmers due to the programming philosophy it supported and continues to support. Python aimed to be simple, whereas other high-level programming languages aimed to be more complex. Pearl is a great example of how this philosophy was applied and how it complicated many things for an average programmer.

Python core developers encouraged early Python adopters to adhere to a simple set of well-known principles known as "The Zen of Python" to write code that both works and looks good. Even after twenty years, these principles are still relevant for Python programmers, and every Python programmer should be aware of them.

Enter the Python code below on the terminal to read all of these principles.

Terminal Code:

```
$ import this
```

We will go over some fundamental principles in order to better understand the philosophy that Python promotes to developers.

- Beautiful Is Better Than Ugly.

All Python programmers are encouraged to write semantically symmetrical code that is also visually appealing. Beautiful code must be well-structured; thus, programmers must write conditionals without complicating the code. Many lines of code can be made more visually appealing by employing indentation techniques. Beautifying code improves readability and can help to reduce runtime.

- Explicit Is Better Than Implicit.

For whatever reason, many developers try to conceal their programming logic, making it difficult for other programmers to understand. Python opposes this routine and encourages developers to write explicit code logic that is understandable by all. This is also one of the reasons why open-source Python frameworks and libraries are more popular.

- Simple Is Better Than Complex.

Your primary goal as a Python programmer should be to write simple code. Simplifying your code logic can help you improve your programming language skills. Your ability to write less complex code improves as you gain experience.

- Complex Is Better Than Complicated.

As with any software, there are times when you need to write complex code that solves multiple problems at once. When working on complex code, avoid making it too complicated. Using exceptions and files effectively can assist you in quickly reducing complicated code that may later turn into annoying bugs.

- There Should Be Only One Approach.

Unlike its predecessor languages, C and C++, Python advocates for consistency. As a Python programmer, you only need to use one logic for all of the instances in your program. Uniformity provides flexibility and makes it easier to maintain the code.

Chapter 3: Python Foundations

Python programmers must ensure that input is provided directly from the user and output is provided based on the inputs in order to have dynamic applications. The Python interpreter and all functions in your program can access the user's input values. We will provide a few example programs in this chapter to help you understand how to improve the user experience of the software you have created based on input and output operations.

Why Are Input Values Required?

Application survival is dependent on input values. Everything runs on the user's input values, from web applications to the most recent metaverse applications. When you log in to Facebook, for example, you must enter your email address and password. These are inputs, and your account will be authenticated only if the information provided is correct.

Face data points are used as input in advanced applications such as facial recognition technology. Nowadays, every real-world application requests and collects user input data in order to provide a better user experience.

Use Cases:

Assume you created a Python application for a mature audience that cannot be used by anyone under the age of 18.

For the above scenario, we can use conditional input verification by asking the user to enter their age. If the user is over the age of 18, the application will become available to him or her. However, if the user is under the age of 18, the application will be inaccessible. Python evaluates whether or not someone can access your software based on inputs from all supported data types. This is just one example from the real world. There are numerous applications that can be performed by utilizing input from your end users.

Understanding the input() Function

When you call the input() function in the middle of a Python program, the interpreter will pause and wait for the user to enter the values using one of their input devices, such as a keyboard, mouse, or mobile touchscreen.

Typically, the user will provide input in response to the prompt. To create real-world applications, you must first create a good prompt GUI. This chapter will look at the text command prompts available to developers.

After entering the values, the user must press the "Enter" button on their system in order for the interpreter to resume and parse the logical programming statements used.

Example:
```
sample = input ("Which country are you from? ")
print (sample + " is a beautiful country!")
```
When the above program is run and executed, the user will first see an output prompt, as shown below.

Output:
```
Which country are you from? United States of America
United States of America is a beautiful country!
```
You can experiment by changing the input above to another country to see what happens.

Output:
```
Which country are you from? France
France is a beautiful country!
```

How To Write User Prompts?

It is recommended to use better prompts to get the user's attention when using the input() function and attempting to receive inputs from the user.

Remember not to include any extraneous information in the text. Make the prompt as straightforward as possible.

Prompt Code:
```
example = input("Which is your favorite hockey team? ")
print ("So you are a " + example + " fan. Hurray!")
```
Output:
```
Which is your favorite football team? Boston Bruins
So you are a Boston Bruins fan. Hurray!
```
You can also use the input() function to prompt the user by displaying multiple lines of strings.

Program Code:
```
prompt = "This is a simple question to find out what you like."
prompt += "\n So, please say your favorite food: "
example = input(prompt)
print (example + " is delicious")
```
Output:
```
This is a simple question to find out what you like.
So, please say your favorite food: Pasta
Pasta is delicious
```
We use the print() function to display text on the screen from the beginning of the book. The only recommended method for printing to a computer screen is print().

Any input you pass to the print() function will be converted to a string literal and displayed on the screen. While you are not required to be aware of the print() function's arguments, learning some parameters that can help you format your code is recommended.

What are String Literals?

String literals are advanced characters that can assist you in quickly formatting your data. For example, \n is a common string literal that can assist you in entering data from a new line.

Other popular string literals that can help you output data with a new tab or without whitespaces and separators are \t, \b, and \d.

What is an End Statement?

The print() function also accepts an end argument, which can be used to append any string data to the end of your string literals, as shown below.

Program Code:

```
print("Italy is a beautiful country. ", end = "Do you agree? ")
print("Yes, I do!")
```

Output:

```
Italy is a beautiful country. Do you agree? Yes, I do!
```

In the above example, "Do you agree?" is the appended text

Comments in Python

When programming teams work on complex and time-consuming projects, a lot of information must be exchanged between team members in order for the project's essence to be understood. Comments allow programmers to pass information without disrupting the program's flow.

When a programmer uses comments, the Python interpreter ignores the comments and moves on to the next line. However, because Python has a large number of open-source projects, comments assist developers in understanding how to integrate third-party libraries and frameworks into their code.

Comments make the code more readable and easier to understand. While it may appear that some programmers do not need to remember the code logic they have written, you would be surprised at how often programmers forget the code logic they have written. Having specific insights into how you wrote the code logic will be very useful for future reference.

Python allows programmers to use two types of comments in their code.

1. Comments on a Single Line

Single-line comments are the most commonly used type of comment by Python programmers because they can be easily written between the lines of code. To use single-line comments, use the '#' symbol. Anything that comes after this symbol will be ignored by the interpreter.

Program Code:

```
# This is an example of a single-line comment followed by a print of a
       hash symbol
print ("This is an example.")
```

Output:

```
This is an example.
```

Because a single-line comment was used, the interpreter ignored it and only executed the print statement.

Why Are Single-Line Comments Important?

Single-line comments are commonly used in the middle of code to assist other programmers in understanding how the program logic works and to detail the functions of the implemented variables.

    2.   Comments in Multiple Lines

While it is possible to write three or four lines of continuous comments using single-line comments, it is not recommended because Python provides a better way to annotate multi-line comments. Python programmers can use string literals to create multi-line comments, as shown below.

Program Code:

```
'''
 This is a comment
 In Python
 with 4 lines
 Author: Python Best '''
print ("This is an example.")
```

Output:

```
This is an example.
```

When you run the above program, only the print statement is executed, just like single-line comments.

Why Are Multiline Comments Important?

Multiline comments are frequently used by programmers to define license details or to explain comprehensive information about various packages and methods with various implementation examples. The code can be effectively understood by the programmers who are reading it.

Reserved Keywords

Reserved keywords are programming language default keywords that programmers cannot use as identifiers while writing code. Identifiers are commonly used to name variables, classes, and functions.

The interpreter will throw an error if you use a reserved keyword in your program. For example, using 'for' for one of your variables will not work because 'for' is typically used in Python programming to define a specific type of loop structure.

There are 33 reserved keywords that you are not permitted to use in your programs. As a Python programmer, it is critical to avoid making unnecessary mistakes when working on complex projects.

Exercise:

Using the Python terminal, try to find the reserved keywords in Python to become familiar with the Python commands we discussed previously.

Operators are commonly used by computer programmers to combine literal and form statements or expressions.

Example:

$$2x + 3z = 34$$

Here, 2x, 3z, and 34 are literals, and + and = are operators that are applied to these literals to form an expression.

Operators in Python

In mathematics, operators are first used to form mathematical expressions. The first programmers used these operators and the basic programming components to easily assign and manipulate values. Operators can be combined with any number of literal values to form complex expressions that can aid programmers in the implementation of difficult algorithms.

Example:

```
a = 18
b = 20
print(a + b)
```

Output:

38

a and b are the operands, whereas = and + are operators that are used.

Different Types of Operators

Different types of operators can be used by programmers to implement various types of programming logic. The most commonly used operators are arithmetic operators, which assist programmers in applying mathematical logic to various literals, such as variables, in their code.

The arithmetic operators that a Python programmer needs to know to write better programming structures are addition, subtraction, multiplication, and division.

1. **Addition**

To add two literals to a program, use the addition operator. These literals can be variables or lists, and they can sometimes be data of two different data types. The

Python interpreter is smart enough to recognize two different data types and return a result to the programmer. The addition operation is represented by the symbol '+'.

Program Code:

```
x = 26
y = 15
z = x + y
# + is the addition operator
print(z)
```

When the program runs using an IDE or IDLE, the interpreter will add the two variable values and assign them to the variable z, as specified by the developer.

Output:

41

2. Subtraction Operator

The subtraction operator is used to subtract two literals. These literals can be variables or lists, and they can sometimes be data of two different data types. - is the symbol for the subtraction operation.

Program Code:

```
x = 26
y = 15
z = x - y
# - is the subtraction operator
print(z)
```

When the program is executed using an IDE or IDLE, the interpreter will find the difference between the two variable values and input it into z as specified by the developer.

Output:

11

3. Multiplication Operator

The multiplication operator computes the product of two literals. These literals can be variables or lists, and they can sometimes be data of two different data types. The symbol * represents a multiplication operation.

Program Code:

```
x = 6
y = 4
z = x * y
# * is the multiplication operator
print(z)
```

When the program runs in an IDE or IDLE, the interpreter will find the product of the two variable values and enter it into the z variable as specified by the developer.

Output:
```
24
```
4. Division Operator

In a program, the division operator is used to find the division quotient of two literals. The quotient can also be calculated using floating-point numbers, and the division symbol "/" is used.

Program Code:
```
x = 8
y = 4
z = x / y
# / is the division operator
print(z)
```
When the program runs in an IDE or IDLE, the interpreter will find the quotient of the two variable values and enter it into the z variable as specified by the developer.

Output:
```
2.0
```
5. Modulus

Modulus is typically used to calculate the remainder of a division operation. The modulus operator can be used to implement a wide range of programming logic, and% is the modulus operation symbol.

Program Code:
```
x = 9
y = 4
z = x % y
# % is the modulus operator
print(z)
```
When the program is executed using an IDE or IDLE, the interpreter will find the remainder of the two variable values and input them into z as specified by the developer.

Output:
```
1
```
The quotient, in this case, is 2.25, but the remainder is 1, as shown in the program output. You can use floor division operations instead of displaying floating-point numbers as a quotient for division operations.

6. Floor Division

Floor division is an alternative arithmetic operator that developers frequently use when they are not concerned with the precision of the result. The nearest integer for the quotient obtained after a division operation is usually displayed by this operator. "//" is the symbol for a floor division operator.

Program Code:

```
x = 9
y = 4
z = x // y
# This is the floor division operator
print (z)
```

Output:

```
2
```

The above program has a Quotient of 2.25. However, because we are using the floor division operator, the program has returned the nearest integer.

7. Bitwise Operators

Bitwise operators are advanced operators that developers frequently use to perform special features such as compression, encryption, and error detection.

Bitwise operators of various types are used in all high-level programming languages.

1. AND (&)
2. OR (|)
3. XOR (^)
4. NOT (~)

All these bitwise operators follow the same principles as logical operators in mathematics.

Operator Precedence

Because there are different operators and mathematical expressions are formed by combining them, dealing with advanced mathematical expressions to create real-world applications can quickly become complex. Operator precedence provides programmers with clear objectives for prioritizing which operators perform a mathematical operation.

If a developer fails to follow operator precedence rules, the values may change completely, resulting in application crashes.

Operator Precedence Rules in Python:

- In any mathematical expression you deal with in Python, precedence takes precedence. As a result, if operators are enclosed by parenthesis, the interpreter will address them first and then move on to the others.
- Bitwise operators are usually given second precedence.
- The mathematical operators used for multiplication and division are given the highest priority. The operators that must be preferred in the same order are *, /, %, and //.
- The remaining arithmetic operations, such as addition and subtraction, take precedence. These operators are represented by the symbols + and -.
- Comparison and logical operators have final operator precedence.

Exercises

1. Create a program that asks the user for two numbers and performs addition, subtraction, multiplication, and division operations using these numbers. Print the results of each operation.

2. Create a program that asks the user for two numbers and checks if the first number is equal to, greater than, or less than the second number. Print the results of each comparison.

3. Create a program that asks the user for three numbers and checks if all of them are positive, or at least one of them is negative. Print the result of the logical operation.

4. Create a program that asks the user for three numbers and check for each number if it is divisible by 3, 4, or 7. Print the result each time.

5. Write a program that asks the user to input two numbers and then performs both a modulus and floor division operation on those numbers. Print the results of both operations to the screen.

Chapter 4: Python Variables

To function properly, Python programs require basic components like variables and operators. These elements, including variables and operators, are simple for novice programmers to comprehend and apply, allowing them to develop algorithms necessary for creating sophisticated software.

What are Variables in Python?

Variables are a way to store and handle data in a Python program. They allow both users and the software to interact with the data. Without data, software applications are useless and serve no purpose for end-users.

Variables are used in Python to store data in a specific computer memory location, allowing the software to upload or download data. The concept of variables was first used in Algebra and has been a fundamental part of high-level programming languages since their inception.

For example, in the mathematical equation $2x + 3y$, the variables x and y can be assigned values, which can then be used to change the output of the equation. In programming, variables with unchanging values are referred to as constants. To understand how variables work in Python, it's important to understand the execution of Python programs, which can be demonstrated through a print statement.

In the same way, by using variables, you can modify the output of a program by supplying literal values. Variables are replaceable, while values that shouldn't be replaced are often referred to as constants in programming.

To grasp how variables function, one needs to comprehend the execution process of Python programs. A print statement will help illustrate this.

Example:

Program Code:

```
print("This is a sentence.")
```

Output:

```
This is a sentence.
```

The code instantly displays the output once the print statement is executed. But there is much more happening behind the scenes.

What happens?

- The program reads each line and matches it with the libraries it has access to.
- An interpreter performs this matching process, using high parsing abilities to identify each character in the program, match variable details, and retrieve information from memory locations to validate the program's logic.

- Despite complex parsing, the program will raise errors if the interpreter cannot find defined methods or variables.
- In the above example, the interpreter recognizes the print statement as a core library method in Python and outputs any string literals in parenthesis.

If you understand the explanation, it is now time to learn about variables in Python.

Program Code:
```
program = " This is a sentence."
print (program)
```
Output:
```
This is a sentence.
```

What Happened?
- At the onset of the program execution, the interpreter will typically parse every line of code given by the programmer.
- Instead of just encountering a print statement followed by text, the interpreter now sees a special identifier referred to as a variable named 'program.' The interpreter checks prior code and discovers that the variable is defined with text and saved at a specific memory location.
- Subsequently, the interpreter will display the variable on the screen as directed by the programmer by retrieving the information defined within the variable.
- This is the fundamental process by which variables work, even in complicated code logic.

Variables can change instantly when they are substituted. It is important for a Python programmer to be aware of this because dynamic programs frequently alter variables according to user inputs and replace them even as the program operates in real time.

Program Code:
```
sample = "My first example"
print(sample)
sample = "My second example"
print(sample)
```
Output:
```
My first example
My second example
```

Since we know that the Python interpreter parses the code line by line sequentially, the first statement in the previous example is printed with the first variable value provided, and the second print statement is printed with the second variable value provided.

How to Name Variables

When creating variables, all Python programmers must follow the Python community's default guidelines. Failure to follow these conditions will result in difficult-to-ignore errors or, in rare cases, application crash. Using a specific guideline when developing programs can also help to improve readability.

Rules to keep in mind:

- Python guidelines specify that variable names can only contain numbers, alphabetical characters, and an underscore. So, for example, 'sample1' can be used as a variable name, whereas '$sample1' cannot because it begins with the unsupported symbol $.
- Python programmers can't begin a variable name with a number. For example, 'sample1' is a valid variable naming format, whereas '1sample' is not.
- Python programmers can't use reserved words assigned to various Python programming routines. Currently, developers cannot use 33 reserved keywords as identifiers when developing real-world Python applications. For example, the keyword 'for' is reserved.
- While this is not a hard and fast rule, it is always preferable to use a simple variable naming method for improved readability. Using complex or confusing variable names can make your code appear sloppy. While this is a good practice for other high-level languages such as C, C++, and Pearl, Python does not support it.

How to Define Variables

All variables defined in the Python programming language begin with the assignment operator (=) to assign a value to the variable.

Syntax Format:

    Name_of_the_variable = Value_of_the_variable

Example:

```
example = 123
# This is a variable with an integer data type
example1 = "USA"
# This is a variable with a string data type
```

In this case, "example" is the name of the variable we created, and 343 is the variable value we assigned to it when it was created.

Consider the variable-defining method above, where we did not explicitly mention any variable data type because Python is intelligent enough to understand variable data types on its own.

How to Determine the Memory Address of a Variable

All variables are kept in a separate memory location. The Python interpreter will pull the information from this memory location whenever you call the variable name. When you ask the Python interpreter to replace a variable, it will simply take the previously placed variable value and replace it with the new variable value. The old variable value will be deleted or saved for future use cases using a garbage mechanism.

Pointers are commonly used in programming languages such as C to quickly determine and pull information about a variable's memory location. Python, on the other hand, does not support pointers because it is often difficult to implement and requires many compilation skills that the interpreter is usually unaware of. Instead, Python developers can use the built-in id() function to quickly obtain the variable's memory address.

Program Code:

```
# First, let's create a variable with an integer data type
sample = 32
# Now let's call its memory address using the built-in function id()
address = id(sample)
print(address)
```

Output:

```
1x10744488x
```

In this case, 1x10744488x is the variable's hexadecimal memory location.

Using the method below, you can now replace the variable and see if the id() has changed.

Program Code:

```
# Let's assign a value to the variable 'sample' and print its address
sample = 64
print(id(sample))
# Now we replace the variable value with a new one
sample = 78
# This will again print the output of the memory location address
print(id(sample))
```

Output:

```
1x10744488x
1x10744488x
```

Although the memory location did not change, a small print verification (print(sample)) is sufficient to see that the variable value has changed.

Local and Global Variables

Variables can be both local and global, depending on your programming logic. Local variables, in theory, can only be used in the methods or classes that you specify. Global variables, on the other hand, can be used in any part of the program without issue. When you call a local variable outside of a function, the Python interpreter will usually throw an error.

Program Code:

```
# This is an example of a local variable within a function
def mysample():
    x = "This is a sentence"
    print(x)
mysample()
```

Output:

```
This is a sentence
```

In this example, the variable is defined as a local variable within a function. As a result, whenever you call it from within a function, it will throw a traceback error, as shown below.

Program Code:

```
# This is an example of a function with a local variable
def sample():
    x = "This is a sentence"
    print(x)
# This is another function
def secondsample():
    print(example)

sample()
secondsample()
```

Output:

```
This is a sentence
NameError: name 'x' is not defined
```

Global variables, on the other hand, can be used to initiate variables for the entire program.

Program Code:

```
# Let's create a global variable
x = "This is a sentence"

# Let's initialize two methods
def method1():
    print(x)
```

```
def method2():
    print(x)

# Let's call them
method1()
method2()
```

Output:

```
This is a sentence
This is a sentence
```

Since both functions can access global variables, two print statements are displayed on the computer screen.

It is entirely up to you to decide which type of variables to use. Many programmers rely heavily on local variables to make their applications run faster. Global variables, on the other hand, can be used if you don't want to be overwhelmed with memory management.

Chapter 5: **Data Types in Python**

Python programmers use a wide range of data types to build cross-platform applications. As a result, a Python programmer must understand the significance of data types in software development.

What exactly are Data Types?

To be more specific, data types are a set of predefined values that programmers use when creating variables. It is also important to remember that because Python is not a statically typed language, it is not necessary to explicitly define variable data types. All statically typed languages, such as C and C++, typically require programmers to define variable data types.

While Python programmers are not required to define them in order to create programs, understanding the various available data types is still necessary for developing complex programs that can interact with users efficiently.

Here's an example of a statically typed language and how variables are defined.

Program Code:

```
int years = 12;
```

In this case, int is the defined data type, years is the variable's name, and 12 is the value supplied to be stored in the age variable.

Python, on the other hand, defines a variable without explicitly defining the variable type, as illustrated below.

Program Code:

```
years = 12
```

years and value are provided here. However, the data type is not defined because the Python interpreter understands that the value provided is an integer.

Different Data Types

Before we get into the various data types that Python supports, let's talk about the basic programming fragments that developers use to create logical statements while programming.

Let's see a simple expression and statement. To make logical statements in a programming language, three main components are used.

1. **Data identifiers**

To store data, programming components such as variables, lists, and tuples are created.

For example:

```
a = 24
```

x is a variable in this programming fragment that was created to store sequential data.

2. Literals

These are the values assigned to any data fragments created by a program.

For Example:

```
a = 24
```

In this programming fragment, **24** is the literal assigned to the newly created data fragment.

3. Operators

Operators implement mathematical operations while developing code for real-world applications.

For Example:

```
a = 24
```

The assignment operator = is used in the preceding code. Other arithmetic operators, such as +, -, *, and /, are well-known for producing logical Python code.

We'll go over some of the most common data types used by Python programmers in their applications.

Strings

Strings are data types that are commonly used to represent a large amount of text. String data types, for example, can be used to represent text in a program by linking them with single quotes. When a string data type is created, an 'str' object with a sequence of characters is created.

Text messages are the most common way for humans to communicate with one another. As a result, strings are the most important data types for developers to understand in order to create meaningful software. It is also critical to represent data in strings because computers only understand binary data. As a result, using ASCII and Unicode encoding mechanisms is critical.

Python 3 introduced an advanced encoding mechanism for understanding foreign languages such as Chinese, Japanese, and Korean, making Strings indispensable for software development.

In what way are strings represented?

```
z = 'This is my sentence'
print (z)
```

Output:

```
This is my sentence
```

Everything between the single quotation marks is a string data type. The variable 'x' is used to define this string data. The number of bits a variable occupies usually determines its memory location and size when it has a string data type. A string data type's number of characters is directly proportional to its bit count.

In the previous example, 'This is an example' has 18 characters, including whitespaces.

As a Python programmer, you have several other options for defining strings. When working on real-world projects, use a single type whenever possible for consistency.

Program Code:

```python
# Double quotes to define strings
a = "This is my sentence"
print(a)


# Three single quotes to define strings
b = '''This is my sentence'''
print(b)


# Three double quotes to define strings
c = """This is my sentence
 but with more than one line """
print(c)
```

Output:

```
This is my sentence
This is my sentence
This is my sentence
 but with more than one line
```

In the previous example, we defined three methods for defining strings. Special characters, symbols, and new tab lines can also be used between quotes. Python also supports escape sequences, which are used by all programming languages. For example, n is a popular escape sequence used by programmers to create new lines.

How Do I Access Characters in Strings?

Because strings are the most commonly used data types in Python, the core library includes several built-in functions for interacting with string data. To access characters in a string, you must first know the index numbers. Index numbers typically begin with 0 rather than 1. Negative indexing and slicing operations can also be used to access a portion of a string.

Example:

```python
# We first create a string to access its characters
s = 'PYTHON'


# We print the whole string
print ('Whole string =', s)


# We print the first character
print ('1st character =', s[0])
```

```
# We print the last character using negative indexing
print ('Last character =', s[-1])

# We print the last character using positive indexing
print ('Again, Last character =', s[5])

# We print the first 2 characters (index 0 to 1)
print ('Sliced character =', s[0:2])
```
Output:
```
Whole string = PYTHON
1st character = P
Last character = N
Again, Last character = N
Sliced character = PY
```
Because all string data types are immutable, it is impossible to replace characters in a literal string. As a result, attempting to replace string characters will result in a Type error.

Program Code:
```
s = 'PYTHON'
s[1] = 'c'
print(s)
```
Output:
```
TypeError: 'str' object does not support item assignment
```

String Formatting

With the modulus (%) operator, Python makes it simple to format your string. It is known as *string formatting operator*.

Program Code:
```
print ("Today I have eaten %d apples" %3)
```
Output:
```
Today I have eaten 4 apples
```
You can use %d to format integers. You can also use %s to format your text.

String Manipulation Techniques

Because strings are the most commonly used data type, the Python core library provides several manipulation techniques for programmers to use. Understanding string manipulation techniques will help you quickly extract data from a large pool of data. These techniques are more widely known among data scientists.

1. Concatenate

Concatenation is the joining of two distinct entities. Using the arithmetic operator '+,' two strings can be joined together using this procedure. If you want to improve string readability, simply use whitespaces between the two strings.

Program Code:
```
example = 'Today is' + 'a wonderful day'
print (example)
```
Output:
```
Today isa wonderful day
```
Remember that whitespaces are not allowed when concatenating. While concatenating, you must add whitespaces on your own, as shown below.

Program Code:
```
example = 'Today is' + ' ' + 'a wonderful day'
print (example)
```
Output:
```
Today is a wonderful day
```

2. Multiply

When you use the String multiply technique, your string value is continuously repeated. The * operator can be used to multiply string content.

Program Code:
```
example = 'Yes '* 4
print(example)
```
Output:
```
Yes Yes Yes Yes
```

3. Appending

You can use this operation to add any string to the end of another string by using the arithmetic operator +=. Keep in mind that the appended string will only be added at the end of the string, not in the middle.

Program Code:
```
example = "Today is a beautiful day "
example += "to start learning Python!"
print (example)
```
Output:
```
Today is a beautiful day to start learning Python!
```

4. Length

In addition to string operations, you can use prebuilt functions in the core library to perform additional tasks in your code. The 'length()' function, for example, returns the number of characters in a string.

Blank Space will be added as a character in the string as well.

Program Code:
```
x = 'Tomorrow it will be sunny'
print(len(x))
```
Output:
```
25
```

5. Find

When you use strings as your primary data type, there will be times when you need to find a specific part of the string. To solve this problem, you can use the built-in find() function. The output will provide an index for the position the first time the input is found so you can verify.

When you use the find() function in Python, the interpreter will only return positive indexes.

Program Code:
```
x = 'Tomorrow it will be sunny'
y = x.find('it')
print(y)
```
Output:
```
9
```

If the substring is not found, the interpreter will return a value of -1.

Program Code:
```
x = 'Tomorrow it will be sunny'
y = x.find('hi')
print(y)
```
Output:
```
-1
```

6. Lower and upper case

lower() and higher() functions can be used to convert characters in a string to completely lower or upper case.

Program Code:
```
example = "Asia is the biggest continent"
sample = example.lower()
print(sample)
```
Output:
```
asia is the biggest continent
```

Program Code:
```
example = "Asia is the biggest continent"
sample = example.upper()
print(sample)
```
Output:
```
ASIA IS THE BIGGEST CONTINENT
```
    7. Title

To convert string format to camel case format, use the title() function.

Program Code:
```
example = "Asia is the biggest continent"
sample = example.title()
print(sample)
```
Output:
```
Asia Is The Biggest Continent
```

Integers

In Python, integers are special data types that allow you to include integer numbers in your code. To perform arithmetic operations or to provide information about a statistical value, numerical values are required.

When a Python interpreter encounters a data value of the integer type, it creates an int object with the value provided. Because int object values are not immutable, they can be replaced whenever the developer desires.

'Int' data types are used by developers to create a variety of complex features in their software. Integers are commonly used to represent the pixel density value of an image or video file.

It is important for a developer to understand the unary operators (+,-), which can be used to represent positive and negative integers, respectively. The unary operator does not need to be specified for positive integers (+), but it must be included for negative integers.

Program Code:
```
x = 13
y = -92
print(x)
print(y)
```
Output:
```
13
-92
```

Python can handle numbers with up to ten digits. While most real-world applications do not cause bottlenecks due to larger numerical values, it's better to be sure that no huge integers are involved.

Floating—Point numbers

All numerical values are not integers. You may occasionally need to work with data with a decimal value. Python ensures that developers deal with this data using floating-point numbers. With floating-point numbers, you can work with decimal values up to ten decimal points long.

Program Code:

```
x = 3.121212
y = 58.4545
print(x)
print(y)
```

Output:

```
3.121212
58.4545
```

Floating-point numbers can also be used to represent data in hexadecimal notation.

Program Code:

```
x = float.hex(15.2698)
print(x)
```

Output:

```
0x1.e8a2339c0ebeep+3
```

Floating-point data types are also commonly used by Python programmers to represent complex and exponential numbers.

Boolean Data Type

Booleans are special data types that are typically used to represent a True or False value when comparing two different values.

Program Code:

```
A = 21
B = 55
print (A > B)
```

Output:

```
False
```

Because the value of A is not greater than the value of B in the preceding example, the output is False. When dealing with logical operations, Boolean data types come in handy.

Chapter 6: Advanced Data Structures in Python

Python programmers frequently deal with large amounts of data, so using variables all the time is not a good idea. Data Scientists, in particular, who frequently deal with large amounts of data, may become overwhelmed by the volume of dynamic data they must deal with. As a result, when working on complex and data-intensive projects, it is critical to use the lists option provided by Python's core library. These are similar to data structures such as arrays found in core programming languages such as C and C++.

Understanding the various data structures provided by Python, as well as learning techniques to add or modify data using these data structures, is a must for any Python programmer.

Lists

Lists are Python data types that allow you to add different data types sequentially. Lists have all of the same properties as variables. They can be easily replaced, passed, or manipulated with the help of the Python core library's methods.

In Python, lists are typically represented as follows:

[22, 23, 24]

The list elements here are 22, 23, and 24. It is also important to understand that all list elements are of integer data type and are not explicitly defined because the Python interpreter can detect their data type.

In the above format, lists begin and end with a square bracket. A comma will be used to separate all of the elements in the list. It's also worth noting that if the elements in a list are of the string data type, they're usually surrounded by quotes. All of the elements in a list are also referred to as items.

Example:

[Alaska, California, Alabama]

Alaska, California, and Alabama are referred to as list elements in this context. As an example, all of the lists can be assigned to a variable. When you print the variable, the list will be printed like any other data type.

Program Code:

```python
x = ['Alaska', 'California', 'Alabama']
print(x)
```

Output:
```
['Alaska', 'California', 'Alabama']
```

Empty List

If a Python list has no elements, it is referred to as an empty list. An empty list is also known as a null list. It's usually written as [].

Program Code:
```
# This is an empty list
emptylist = []
```

List Indexing

Python makes it simple to manipulate or replace the elements of a list, specifically through the use of indexes. Indexes typically begin with 0 and provide Python programmers with numerous functions, such as "slicing" and "searching," to ensure that their programs run smoothly.

Assume we have a list that we have previously used. We will print each element on the computer screen using the indexes.

Program Code:
```
myList = ['California', 'Alaska', 'Alabama']
print(myList[0])
print(myList[1])
print(myList[2])
```

Output:
```
'California'
'Alaska'
'Alabama'
```

In the previous example, when the Python interpreter detects 0 as an index, it prints the first element. As the index rises, so does the position on the list.

The items in the list can also be called as shown below, along with a string literal.

Program Code:
```
myList = ['California', 'Alaska', 'Alabama']
print(myList [1] + ' is a wonderful state')
```

Output:
```
California is a wonderful state
```

If you provide an index value that is greater than the number of list elements present, an index error will be returned.

Program Code:
```
myList = ['California', 'Alaska', 'Alabama']
print(myList [3])
```

Output:
```
IndexError: list index out of range
```

Note: It is also important to remember that the floating-point number cannot be used as an index value.

Program Code:
```
myList = ['California', 'Alaska', 'Alabama']
print(myList [2.2])
```
Output:
```
TypeError: list indices must be integers or slices, not float
```
As shown below, all lists can have other lists as elements. Child lists are all the lists contained within a list.

Program Code:
```
x = [[5,123,4],56,32,14]
print(x)
```
Output:
```
[[5, 123, 4], 56, 32, 14]
```
You can call the elements in the child list using the 'list [][]' format.

Program Code:
```
x = [[5,123,4],56,32,14]
print(x[0][1])
```
Output:
```
123
```
In the previous example, the second element of the nested list is 123, which is displayed as output. The elements of a list can also be referred to using the negative index. Typically, -1 denotes the last index, whereas -2 denotes the element preceding the last element.

Program Code:
```
myList = ['California', 'Alaska', 'Alabama']
print(myList [-1])
```
Output:
```
Alabama
```
You've already learned about how lists are represented. In the following section, we will discuss some of the functions that can be manipulated using a list data structure.

Slicing Using Lists

Slicing lists allows programmers to avoid dealing with an overwhelming number of elements contained within a list. By slicing, you can focus only on the part of a list that is relevant to your program logic.

Syntax:

Listname[start of the index : end of the index]

A colon is typically used to separate the beginning and ending indexes of the list that you want to slice.

Program Code:
```
myList = [23,34,78,94,54]
print(myList[1:3])
```
Output:
```
[34, 78]
```
You do not need to enter the list's beginning or end when slicing the list elements. If it is not entered, the interpreter will assume it is the first or last element in the list.

Program Code:
```
myList = [23,34,78,94,54]
print(myList[:3])
```
Output:
```
[23, 34, 78]
```
Because the slice value before the semicolon was not provided in the previous example, the interpreter assumed it came from the first element.

Program Code:
```
myList = [23,34,78,94,54]
print(myList[3:])
```
Output:
```
[94, 54]
```
In this example, the interpreter has assumed that the value following the semicolon represents the end of the list. If neither value is provided, the entire list is returned, as shown below.

Program Code:
```
myList = [23,34,78,94,54]
print(myList[:])
```
Output:
```
[23, 34, 78, 94, 54]
```
Get list length
To quickly determine the length of a list, use the built-in len() function.

Program Code:
```
myList = [23,34,78,94,54]
print(len(myList))
```
Output:
```
5
```

Changing Values of a List
As shown below, you can easily change the values inside a list using the assignment operator.

Program Code:
```
myList = [23,34,78,94,54]
myList [3] = 58
```

```
print(myList)
```
Output:
```
[23, 34, 78, 58, 54]
```
You can also replace a list value with an already existing list value, as shown below.

Program Code:
```
myList = [23,34,78,94,54]
myList [3] = myList[2]
print(myList)
```
Output:
```
[23, 34, 78, 78, 54]
```

Concatenating Lists

The Arithmetic operator '+' can be used to easily combine two lists.

Program Code:
```
myList = [23,34,78,94,54]
x = [1,2,3]
print(myList + x)
```
Output:
```
[23, 34, 78, 94, 54, 1, 2, 3]
```

Replication of a List

Using the '*' operator, you can quickly multiply list elements with this function.

Program Code:
```
print([1,2,3] * 4)
```
Output:
```
[1, 2, 3, 1, 2, 3, 1, 2, 3, 1, 2, 3]
```

Element Deletion

Using the 'del' statement, you can easily remove an element from a list.

Program Code:
```
myList = [12,13,14,15,16,17]
del(myList [2])
print(myList)
```
Output:
```
[12, 13, 15, 16, 17]
```

Using the operators "in" and "not in"

Using the logical operators 'in' and 'not in,' Python makes it simple to determine whether a list element is present or not in a list. As a result, this function returns either a True or False Boolean value.

Program Code:

```
colors = ['yellow', 'orange', 'blue']
x = 'orange' in colors
print(x)
```

Output:

```
True
```

index()

Using the index() list function, you can quickly determine the index position of a list element.

Program Code:

```
x = [12, 45, 78]
print(x.index(45))
```

Output:

```
1
```

If you provide a list element that does not exist within a list, you will receive a type error.

Program Code:

```
x = [12, 45, 78]
print(x.index(49))
```

Output:

```
ValueError: 49 is not in list
```

insert()

You can insert a new element to the list at any position in the list by using the insert() function.

Syntax:

insert(index position, 'item')

Program Code:

```
x = [12, 45, 78]
x.insert(2,11)
print(x)
```

Output:

```
[12, 45, 11, 78]
```

The third element is moved to the fourth position and the new element is added to the third

sort()

Python developers can easily arrange all the elements in a list using either ascending or descending order by using the sort() function.

Program Code:
```
x = [78, 12, 45]
x.sort()
print(x)
```
Output:
```
[12, 45, 78]
```
If you use strings in the list, the list will be sorted alphabetically.

Program Code:
```
x = ['yellow', 'blue', 'orange', 'grey']
x.sort()
print(x)
```
Output:
```
['blue', 'grey', 'orange', 'yellow']
```

Tuples

Even though lists are popular data structures that Python programmers frequently use in their applications, they have several implementation issues. Because all lists created with Python are mutual objects, they are simple to replace, delete, or manipulate.

As a software developer, you may be required to keep immutable lists that cannot be altered in any way. That's why tuples exist. Within Tuples, it is not possible to change initiated elements in any way. When you try to change the content of a tuple, you will get a "Type Error" message.

Program Code:
```
# Let's create a tuple using Python
t = ('Cat', 'Tree', 'Apple')
print(t)
```
Output:
```
('Cat', 'Tree', 'Apple')
```
In the previous example, we simply initiated a tuple and used a print function to display it on the screen. Tuples, unlike lists, are not represented with square brackets, but rather with parenthesis to distinguish them from lists.

To understand how tuples work, try changing one of the elements in the preceding example and printing the tuple to see what happens.

Program Code:
```
t = ('Cat', 'Tree', 'Apple')
print(t)

# Trying to replace an element in the tuple...
t[2] = 'Mango'
print(t)
```

Output:
```
('Cat', 'Tree', 'Apple')
TypeError: 'tuple' object does not support item assignment
```
In the previous example, if a tuple element is changed, the interpreter will throw an error. This demonstrates that all tuple elements are immutable and cannot be replaced, deleted, or added.

Tuples Concatenation

Tuples, like the many list operations we've seen, can be used to work on specific operations. For example, just like lists, you can use Python to add or multiply the elements in a tuple.

Program Code:
```
tuple1 = (17,18,19)
tuple2 = (16,19,28)
# Adding two tuples
print(tuple1 + tuple2)
```
Output:
```
(17, 18, 19, 16, 19, 28)
```
The Addition operator is used to concatenate two tuples in the preceding example. Similarly, you can use the multiplication operator to quickly increase the elements in your tuple. We can also nest tuples within tuples. This is commonly referred to as nesting tuples.

Program Code:
```
X = (1,2,3)
Y = ('Orange','Apple','Banana')
Z = (X,Y)
print(Z)
```
Output:
```
((1, 2, 3), ('Orange', 'Apple', 'Banana'))
```
Two tuples are nested within another tuple in the previous example.

Replication

When working with lists, you can use the * operator to repeat the values.

Program Code:
```
T = (4,5,6) * 4
print(T)
```
Output:
```
(4, 5, 6, 4, 5, 6, 4, 5, 6, 4, 5, 6)
```
As previously stated, changing the values of tuples is impossible because they are designed to be immutable. Here is what happens if we try to swap one value for another.

Program Code:

```
T = (45,78,89)
T[2] = 15
print(T)
```

Output:

```
TypeError: 'tuple' object does not support item assignment
```

Slicing With Tuples

The slicing technique, which uses indexes to extract a portion of the tuple, makes it simple to slice a portion of the tuple.

Program Code:

```
t = (24,25,26,27,28,29,30)
print(t[2:4] )
```

Output:

```
(26, 27)
```

Tuple Deletion

It is not possible to delete a specific element from a tuple, but it is possible to delete the entire tuple using the command below. This is true for any type of variable.

Program Code:

```
t = (24,25,26,27,28,29,30)
del t
print(t)
```

Output:

```
NameError: name 't' is not defined
```

Dictionaries

values as pairs rather than single values as lists and tuples do. The "key: value" pair is used by dictionaries to ensure that the data provided is more optimized and works better. Dictionaries are also represented by curly brackets, which distinguishes them from lists and tuples.

How Do I Create a Dictionary?

As previously stated, dictionaries are defined using key: value pairs separated by commas. The elements will be placed in sequential order and must be separated.

Syntax:

Dictionary_sample = { key: value , key: value ....) }

As a developer, you can add an unlimited number of key:value pairs to a dictionary.

Example:

```
Capitals = {'France': 'Paris', 'Spain': 'Madrid', 'Italy': 'Rome'}
print(Capitals)
```

Output:

```
{'France': 'Paris', 'Spain': 'Madrid', 'Italy': 'Rome'}
```

You can also build a nested dictionary. A nested dictionary is a dictionary within a dictionary:

```
Capitals = {'France': 'Paris', 'Spain': 'Madrid', 'Italy': 'Rome',
        'Australia': {'Melbourne', 'Sydney'}}
print(Capitals)
```

Output:

```
{'France': 'Paris', 'Spain': 'Madrid', 'Italy': 'Rome', 'Australia':
        {'Sydney', 'Melbourne'}}
```

The last key: pair value in the second example has a dictionary with two key:pair values.

Exercises

1. List exercise: Create a list of 5 numbers and then print the sum and average of the numbers.

2. Create a tuple of 5 names and then print the first and last name.

3. Create a dictionary with 5 key-value pairs and then print the value of the third key.

4. Create a list with 5 fruits (e.g. apples, bananas, etc.). Ask the user to input a fruit. Check if the fruit is in the list. If the fruit is in the list, display a message saying "The fruit is in the list." If the fruit is not in the list, display a message saying "The fruit is not in the list."

5. Create a list with 3 colors. Then ask the user to give a color as input. If the color is in the list, display a message saying so. Otherwise, append the color given by the user to the end of the list and print the updated list

A Note to the Reader

So far, I hope you're enjoying the contents of this book! I have spent time, energy, and money on the creation of this manuscript. That's why I want to make sure that all of my efforts are worthwhile and that you're excited about this new world.

To download the pdf with the Python interview Q&As and the solutions to the exercises, **scan the QR code at the end of the book if you haven't already.**

For any questions, please contact me at phillirobbins.py@gmail.com. I will improve the content of this book to provide better and better quality.
In addition, I encourage you to leave a review on Amazon. It's a friendly thing that will only take a few minutes of your time, but it will mean a lot to me. In fact, for us "independent authors," this is the only way to promote ourselves.

Scan the QR code below to leave a quick Amazon review!

What is the best way to do it? **Upload a short video of yourself discussing your thoughts on the book!**

Is it too much for you? No problem! **You could still write a review with a couple of pictures of the book, that would still be very helpful!**

NOTE: don't feel obliged, but it would be greatly appreciated!

Thanks for your patience and enjoy your reading!

Chapter 7: Conditionals and Loops

Any computer program must make decisions for real-world applications. A mobile application with advanced software, for example, will use your inputs to display whatever you want. While using a mobile or web application, the user makes decisions. The program must be intelligent enough to provide a relevant interface based on the user's selection. This dynamic thinking is very similar to human thinking. When writing in Python, you must be aware of conditionals and loops to ensure that your programs mimic these conditions. These are high-level programming structures that can make your Python programs more effective.

Conditionals and loops can also help you reduce the execution time of your programs, making them run faster. A Python programmer who wants to work with well-known teams should be aware of these techniques, as they are also prerequisite requirements for more advanced topics such as Functions and Modules, which we will discuss further.

Comparison Operators

To practically understand conditionals and loops, you must be aware of the various comparison operators supported by Python as a programming language.

Comparison operators, also known as relational operators, typically compare two operands to each other and return a Boolean value, either True or False.

Note: 'True' and 'False' are special Boolean values supported by Python to assist programs in making relevant decisions. Boolean values are the basic logic gates present within microprocessors.

1. Less than (<) operator

This operator determines whether the left operand value is less than the right operand value.

Program Code:
```
print(12 < 19)
```
Output:
```
True
```
Program Code:
```
print(87 < 36)
```
Output:
```
False
```
If you look at the two examples above, you'll notice that the first has a 'True' output because 12 is less than 19, while the second has a 'False' output because 87 is not less than 36.

With a less-than operator, you can apply the same principle to floating-point values.

Program Code:
```
a = 9.5 < 10.26
print(a)
```

Output:
```
True
```

To compare strings in ASCII format, you can also use the "less than" operator.

Program Code:
```
a = 'Banana' < 'banana'
print(a)
```

Output:
```
True
```

Because the ASCII value of lowercase letters is usually higher than that of uppercase letters, the Boolean value in the previous example is True.

Exercise:

Determine the ASCII sum for the word 'banana' mentioned above.

These relational operators can also be applied to other data structures, such as tuples. Before comparing, however, ensure that all of the values in a tuple are of the same data type.

Program Code:
```
print((15,18,98) < (25,48,18,19))
```

Output:
```
True
```

If the tuples have different data types, an error message will appear on the terminal.

Program Code:
```
print((20,30,40) < ('three',4,5))
```

Output:
```
TypeError: '<' not supported between instances of 'int' and 'str'
```

2. Greater than (>) operator

A *greater than* operator is typically used to determine whether the left operand value is greater than the right operand value.

Program Code:
```
print(32 > 56)
```

Output:
```
False
```

The Boolean value in the first example is False because the right operand value 32 is less than 56.

The same relational operator can also be used with floating-point values and other data types, such as tuples.

3. Equal (== operator)

An *equal* operator determines whether the values of the right and left operands are equal. If the operand values are the same, the Boolean value is True. Otherwise, it's False.

Program Code:
```
print(5 == 5)
```
Output:
```
True
```
Program Code:
```
print(12 == 21)
```
Output:
```
False
```

Control Flow Statements

With a solid understanding of comparison operators under your belt, you are now ready to learn about the various control statements that are required of all Python developers. Control flow statements are commonly used by programmers to write simple code for beginners.

Sequential Structure

All of your program's steps will typically be executed linearly in a sequential structure. As a result, many programs have a sequential structure in order to avoid writing complex code. However, sequential code requires a high level of skill from programmers because developing programming logic in a linear way can be difficult.

Example:
```
a = 6
print (a, "is a perfect number")
```
Output:
```
6 is a perfect number
```
In the previous example, the Python interpreter parsed the code line by line to produce an output.

Conditional Structure

The conditional structure is a well-known programming structure that is used to execute only a portion of the program while ignoring the remaining logical code based on the conditional statements.

Only partial statements are executed in a conditional structure, which allows Python interpreters to save time by not parsing the entire code.

If and if-else conditional structures are two well-known conditional branches used by Python programmers.

Looping Structure

Looping structures are useful when you want to repeat the same statement or programming logic in a program based on logical conclusions. The Python interpreter allows you to repeat a programming step until the condition is met.

To make the most of the looping structure, developers must write both loop-starting and loop-terminating logic. While and for loops are two common looping structures that Python programmers can use in their code.

If/Else Conditional Statements

To perform specific operations, conditional statements rely on fundamental decision-making. If the condition is not met, the conditional logic will skip that particular block. Python includes a basic if/else statement for choosing between two blocks using a logical statement.

Syntax:

    if condition:
            execute statement
        else:
            execute statement

Program Code:

```
x = 31
if x % 4 == 0:
    print("This number is divisible by 4")
else:
        print("This number is not divisible by 4")
```

Output:

```
This number is not divisible by 4
```

Explanation:

- To begin, we must define a variable that will be used when we set up our condition for the if/else conditional.
- Indentation is required for the code that is eventually executed after the if (else) statement.
- Advanced programs use automatic input methods to get values from users.
- After storing the variable, the interpreter will parse the condition used by the if block.
- The Python interpreter will perform a remainder operation to see if the number is divisible by three.
- If it is divisible by three, the block immediately following the if statement should have been executed.
- Because the condition is false, the interpreter will skip the if block and instead execute the statements in the else block, which will result in the output.

Let's see an example of a condition that fulfills the if block.

Program Code:

```
x = 30
if x % 3 == 0:
    print("This number is divisible by 3")
else:
        print("This number is not divisible by 3")
```

Output:

```
This number is divisible by 3
```

If the condition is satisfied the print statement in the if block is executed, and the else block is skipped by the interpreter.

If Elif Else

Using multiple conditional expressions in a single program block allows you to make better use of conditionals.

Program Code:

```
n = 15
if n % 3 == 0:
        print("Number divisible by 3")
elif n % 4 == 0:
        print("Number divisible by 4")
else:
        print("Number not divisible by 3 and 4")
```

Output:

```
Number divisible by 3
```

In the previous example, the Python interpreter must check three conditions. When the Python interpreter determines that the first condition is true, it prints it and ignores the other two.

If any two statements are true, only the first one in the sequence of the code will be printed.

For Loops

Looping structures, like conditionals, are building blocks for Python software. Instead of constantly checking a condition, you can loop it using a for or while loop.

A for loop can be used with any data structure, including lists, tuples, and dictionaries.

Syntax:

```
for i in object:
        { Enter the body of a loop here }
```

When a condition is specified, the for loop can loop through all the items of the data structure.

Example:

```
v = [45,89,56]
out = 0
for val in v:
    out = out + val
print ("Sum of the 3 elements of the vector v:", out)
```

Output:

```
Sum of the 3 elements of the vector v: 190
```

In the previous example, instead of performing arithmetic operations on each element of the list, we simply used a for loop to automate this procedure.

While Loop

While the for loop is great for automating tasks, it can be difficult to write logical code since there is no way to apply a condition to the loop. This is where a while loop comes in handy.

A while loop will be provided prior to looping, with the condition being checked each time the loop occurs.

Syntax:

```
        while condition
                {Enter the statement for a while loop here}
```

Example:

```
a = 0
b = 1
N = int(input("Enter number: "))
while b <= N:
    a = a + b
    b = b + 1
print ("The sum of numbers from 1 to", N, "is", a)
```

Output:

```
Enter number: 10
The sum of numbers from 1 to 10 is 55
```

Conditionals and loops can be nested to create more complex programs.

Break and Continue

Loops can complete a large amount of complex programming logic in a short period of time. While they are useful in many situations, they can consume a lot of run-time memory, causing programs to crash unexpectedly.

To solve this problem, Python provides two programming components known as break and continue.

Break Statement

When the Python interpreter encounters a 'break' in a program, it immediately ends the loop and moves on to the line following the loop. Any time the 'break' occurs inside a loop, the loop will end and the next statements will be executed.

Syntax:

    break

Example Program:

```
M = 10
j = 1
while j <= M:
    if j %2 == 0:
        print (j, "is divisible by 2 ")
    if j % 3 == 0:
        print (j, "is divisible by 3 ")
        break
    j = j + 1
```

Output:

```
2 is divided by 2
3 is divisible by 3
```

When the interpreter reads the break statement in the previous example, the program will end. What would the output be without the 'break'? (hint: all the numbers <= 10 that are divisible by 2 and 3...).

Continue Statement?

When the Python interpreter encounters 'continue' in a program, it immediately ends the loop and moves on to the next iteration. Keep in mind that this statement will not completely end the loop. Proceeding to the next logical statement in a loop will only save time and processing energy.

Example Program:

```
for letter in 'Productivity':
    if letter == 't':
        continue
    print('Letter now:', letter)
```

Output:

```
Letter now: P
Letter now: r
Letter now: o
Letter now: d
Letter now: u
Letter now: c
Letter now: i
Letter now: v
Letter now: i
Letter now: y
```

Exercises

1. Write a program that asks the user for an integer and calculates the factorial of the given number. Use a for loop to accomplish this task.

2. Write a program that counts the number of vowels (a, e, i, o, u) of a string given as input from the user. Loop the string and check if the current character is a vowel.

3. Create some code to produce a random number between 1 and 100. The program should then ask the user to guess the number and keep asking until the user has entered the correct number. Use a while loop to accomplish this task.

4. Write a program that prints the first n even numbers. Ask the user for the value of n. Use a for loop to generate the numbers, and an if statement to determine if the current number is even.

5. Write a program that prints the first n Fibonacci numbers. The Fibonacci sequence is a series of numbers in which each number is the sum of the two preceding ones. The first two numbers in the series are 0 and 1. Use a for loop to generate the numbers and break the loop when n numbers have been printed.

Chapter 8: Functions and Modules

Python supports a variety of programming paradigms. The functional programming paradigm is the most widely used programming paradigm for developers to write code in. Functional programming is adaptable and simple to use for simple projects that require fewer developers to complete the code. Because of the faster implementation of various programming components, the functional paradigm is also considered versatile.

Creating programs with functions may be difficult because you must always call the function within the program. With the help of a few examples, you can learn functional programming and create complex programs with less code.

A Real-World Example:

Functions were first used in mathematics to solve complex problems in discrete mathematics. Later, programmers began implementing this concept in order to reuse previously written code without rewriting it.

Let's use a simple mobile app to demonstrate how functions work in real-world applications.

Picsart is a popular mobile photo editing app that offers a variety of filters and tools for image manipulation. For example, the crop tool makes it simple for users to crop their images. Now, when Picsart developers write code, they typically use a variety of libraries, frameworks, and functions. Cropping, for example, necessitates its own function due to the numerous complex tasks involved in dividing pixels and providing output to the user.

Assume the developers wanted to update the application to include video cropping support. For programmers, there are currently two options.

1. They can design a cropping function from the ground up.
2. They can use the photo cropping function and add additional functionalities.

Many developers prefer option two because it is simpler and saves time. However, as previously stated, creating functions is not as simple. It requires a great deal of complex logic to connect the functions to the core application framework and other third-party libraries.

Types of Functions

System functions and user-defined functions are the two main types of functions.

The core Python library provides system functions, which are frequently used by developers to perform common tasks. 'print,' for example, is a system function that displays a literal string literal on the screen.

Developers, on the other hand, create user-defined functions specifically for their software. Users can also integrate third-party libraries' user-defined functions into their code.

Regardless of the type of code you use, keep in mind that the primary goal of using functions as a programmer is to solve problems with less reusable code.

How Do They Work?

The philosophy behind the use of functions in programming is similar to that of mathematical functions. The developer will first define a function with complex code logic and a name that can be called from anywhere in the program using unique programming components known as parameters. The developers then explicitly define what type of parameters the user can provide for fewer crashes.

If the function is not called, users will be unable to use the code logic that the developer created. Function calling is frequently displayed in the front end via buttons, tabs, and other graphical user interfaces. While it may be as simple as a tap for the end user, a function will be called programmatically in order for a software component to function properly.

How Should You Define Your Functions?

There is no need to define the default system functions because they are built. You can only call them. Even though programmers can modify system functions, doing so is not recommended because they are typically complex, and messing with them will break your code.

Python developers who want to create game-changing software, on the other hand, can use the "def" keyword to create functions.

A simple example is provided to help you understand function declaration in Python more quickly.

Program Code:

```
# Function to print a welcome message
def welcome():
    print ("Good morning, I Hope you are fine.")
welcome()
```

Output:

```
Good morning, I Hope you are fine.
```

Explanation:

- While this is a simple program, its workflow is similar to that of more complex programs. When working on real-world projects, the number of steps only increases.

- First, we use the 'def' keyword in line 1 to initialize a function in the program. If the def keyword is not used, the function will not work because the interpreter will not understand that it is a function.
- The name of the function is defined alongside def. The function is called "welcome" in this case. The same rules apply to naming functions as they do to variables.
- The body of the function is everything that comes after the comment. Variables, functions, and constants can all be part of a function body. The main core logic of the function is usually defined in this body.
- The body of the function is usually preceded by a comment or docstring. We used a comment in this example. When you use two single quotes to provide information about a function, this is referred to as a docstring.

If you are using multiple lines to provide information, then you can use three single quotes.

Example:

```
# This is an example of a function that we are using for beginners
def myFunction():
    '''

    Author: John
    Function: myFunction
    What does it do? It simply prints
    '''

    print ("Hi! I wish you a wonderful day!")


myFunction()
```

The program's third line defines a print statement that displays content on the screen. You can use as many built-in functions as you want in this area to make your program look more natural for the time being. Even though the data is static, it helps you understand how legacy applications work.

The final line shows how the developer invokes a function. In this case, myFunction() is a function call. There are no parameters between parentheses because this is a simple program. Multiple parameters can be used in complex programs. When the interpreter finds a function call, it immediately searches for the function and does whatever the function requests.

Function Parameters

There were no parameters in the previous example function. That is not the case in real-world applications, as programs are frequently complex and difficult to understand. To use functions, you must first create functions that use parameters and perform tasks.

Assume, based on the previous example, that we have two users for our application, and we need to greet them by calling them by their names.

Program Code:
```
def mysample():
# Function that prints the same welcome message to two different users
    print("Hi Sam, I hope you are fine!")
    print("Hi Tom, I hope you are fine!")
mysample()
```

Output:
```
Hi Sam, I hope you are fine!
Hi Tom, I hope you are fine!"
```

To begin, create two print statements that use both input/conditionals and print statements to validate the user and display the correct output. This is overly complicated and unnecessary, as parameters can assist you in creating dynamic welcome messages for your users. Not just for two, but for thousands of users, with just a minor change when creating a function.

Consider this example function with a single parameter that can assist you in creating a dynamic message.

Program Code:
```
# This is an example function with a single parameter
def mysample(name):
    print ("Hi " + name + ". " + "How are you doing?")
mysample('Sam')
mysample('Tom')
mysample('John')
mysample('Mike')
```

Output:
```
Hi Sam. How are you doing?
Hi Tom. How are you doing?
Hi John. How are you doing?
Hi Mike. How are you doing?
```

Explanation:
- A function named 'mysample' is created, and the parameter 'name' is defined between parenthesis. Because the Python interpreter is intelligent enough to parse any data value provided by the user, you may not need to specify the data type for this parameter.
- The programmer used the arithmetic operator to divide the string after calling the parameter in the print function. As a result, whenever the user enters data, it is placed between the default strings.

- In the following lines, the developer has called the function with the parameter input. For complex applications, the parameter cannot be fixed and must be provided by the user. We used the default parameters in this example. The parameters provided by the developer are Sam, Tom, John, and Mike.

If you want to start creating more advanced functions, you can use Python's argument functionality.

Arguments of a Function

To fully utilize their capabilities, all modern applications use variables for the functions. In the previous example program, we used default arguments for the function parameter. However, for Python developers, always providing parameters by default is not ideal. Users can pass arguments to the function through all parameters. While there are several ways to pass arguments to function parameters, the most common are positional and keyword arguments.

Positional Arguments

When using positional arguments, programmers typically provide the values for the function parameters directly. It may appear to be perplexing, but many programmers use it since it is easier to implement. It is essential to remember the order in which positional arguments are passed.

Program Code:

```python
def age(who, years):
    '''
    This function states the age of different people
    '''
    print(who, "is", years, "years old")


age('Mike', 35)
age('Tom', 24)
```

Output:

```
Mike is 35 years old
Tom is 24 years old
```

The arguments for the first instance in the previous example are 'Mike' and 35. Because no data types are specified, the Python interpreter will determine the value type and throw it to the function.

Parameter names are important because there is no direct way to understand the data type that we are using. A name is represented by a literal string, while a number is represented by an integer data type. A comma is typically used to separate all the arguments.

It is easy to make mistakes when using positional arguments, as demonstrated below.

Program Code:

```
def age(who, years):
    print(who, "is", years, "years old")


age(35, 'Mike')
age(24, 'Tom')
```

Output:

```
35 is Mike years old
24 is Tom years old
```

While the function produces an output, it is incorrect because the arguments are for opposite parameters.

Keyword Arguments can be used to define function parameters to solve these minor issues with positional arguments.

Keyword Arguments

With keyword arguments, you can directly pass arguments to the function parameter. Keyword arguments use parameter = value format to give arguments to any function. Keyword Arguments cause less confusion but take more time to implement and hence are not often used by developers working on complex projects that involve a lot of code.

Program Code:

```
def age(who, years):
    print(who, "is", years, "years old")


age(who = 'Mike', years = 35)
age(years = 24, who = 'Tom')
```

Output:

```
Mike is 35 years old
Tom is 24 years old
```

The format in which keyword arguments are defined here is *parameter = argument*. In *who = 'Mike'*, for example, *who* is the parameter and *Mike* is the argument.

Default Values

Not all values in a Python or other programming language program must be dynamic. Default values, also known as 'constants,' are sometimes used by developers when passing arguments to a function. Using default values for parameters is completely optional for programmers.

However, defining default values is recommended because it reduces boilerplate code and offers better data management if the project is complex. Boilerplate code is unnecessary, but it must be written by developers for the interpreter to function properly. While Python is clutter-free in comparison to other high-level languages, some changes to the code, such as defining default values, are required to improve code readability.

Program Code:

```python
def age(who, years = 35):
    print(who, "is", years, "years old")


age('Mike')
age('Tom')
```

Output:

```
Mike is 35 years old
Tom is 35 years old
```

Because we have already defined a parameter value in the previous example, function calling becomes easier and takes less time.

It is important to remember that even if you have given the default value, the Python interpreter will end up replacing the argument if it is defined again.

Program Code:

```python
def age(who, years = 35):
    print(who, "is", years, "years old")


age('Mike')
age('Tom', 24)
```

Output:

```
Mike is 35 years old
Tom is 24 years old
```

Despite the fact that the default value is 35, the argument for Tom is given as 5. In this case, the Python interpreter replaces it with the new argument value.

Scope

"Scope" is critical for developers to understand the various types of functions available and to find ways to use them without difficulty. Functions, like variables, have a local scope and a global scope, as previously explained.

Local scope variables are all variables created within a function that can only be used within it. By contrast, any variable that can be used is referred to as a global scope variable.

Remember that a function can have both local and global variables. As a result, all variables used in the function should be either local or global.

Why Is Scope Crucial?

The scope functionality is mostly used to maintain the garbage mechanism more effectively. To increase the program's speed, all variables that have been replaced or have not been used in a long time are usually destroyed. While they can be recreated when the function is called, the process still consumes runtime.

Instead, when a variable with global scope is created, it will probably be called multiple times. Therefore, having a global scope is useful to avoid the need to reinitialize variables. Regardless of the software you are creating, using scope whenever possible can help you increase your efficiency while working on complex projects.

Local and Global Scope

Rule—1: Local Scope Variables Cannot Be Used in a Global Scope
Program Code:
```
def mysample():
    x = 12


mysample()
print(x)
```
Output:
```
NameError: name 'x' is not defined
```
The previous example declares a variable with a local scope and a value of 12. When we call the function and attempt to print the variable value from the global scope, we get a traceback error because local variables, unlike global variables, can only be called within a function.

Program Code:
```
def mysample():
    x = 12
    print(x)
mysample()
```
Output:
```
12
```
Because the function is called from the local scope, the program runs without error and prints the local variable to the computer screen using the print statement.

Rule—2: Regardless of their scope, all local functions can use all variables.
Program Code:
```
x = 23
def mysample():
    y = 45
    print(x)
mysample()
print(x)
# print(x) would produce an error
```

Output:
```
23
23
```
When the variable is called from the local and global scopes, the value of the variable 'x' is printed.

Rule—3: Local variables that are used by one function can't be used by another.
Program Code:
```
def f1():
    x = 12
    print(x)
f1()

def f2():
    print(x)
f2()
```
Output:
```
24
NameError: name 'x' is not defined
```
Because it is a variable from the local function, the print function works for the first time. The variable value, on the other hand, causes a traceback error for the second time because the function 'f2' can't access the variable of the function 'f1'.

It should be noted that variables in both the local and global scopes can have the same name without causing confusion. However, for better programming practice and to avoid confusion, it is recommended that local and global variables be given different names.

Modules

In a programming language, a module is a group of functions. You can use these groups of functions in any software component by simply importing the module and calling the function with your parameters as arguments.

Python imports modules much better than traditional languages like C and C++. Many programmers import modules in order to use the module's methods and add additional capabilities on top of it.

Syntax:

   import { Name of the module }
Example:
```
import math
```
The syntax above will import all the built-in math module functions into your program. As a result, you can now present your arguments for these methods.

What is the function of Import?

Import is a Python library function that copies all the functions in a specific file and links them to the current file. In this way, you can use methods that aren't in the current file. Furthermore, creating modules is useful to avoid writing the same code over and over again.

How Do I Create Modules?

While importing modules from third-party libraries saves time, as a developer, you must be aware of the importance of creating modules on your own.

Assume you're developing a web application for a torrent service. It would be beneficial if you wrote a large number of functions to make the application work. To improve organization, it will be better to create a networking module and include all networking-related functions in it. Following that, you can create a module with a GUI and several functions to aid in the creation of a visually appealing application.

To begin creating a Python module, you must first create a text file with the.py extension. After you've created the.py file, you can now add all the functions to it. For example, in the.py module we just created, you could include the following function to multiply two numbers.

File – examplemodule.py

```
def sum(a,b):
# This method computes the sum of two numbers
c = a * b
return c
# The sum will be the output
```

We will show a sample script that imports the previous function as the module is created.

Program Code:

```
import examplemodule
```

After pressing the enter key, the functions in that module will be available to a Python programmer working on other projects.

Program Code:

```
examplemodule.sum(12,23)
```

Output:

```
35
```

The script will automatically detect the 'sum' function, and the sum will be displayed on the computer screen based on the arguments provided.

Modules and Built-In Functions

While creating complex and complicated software applications, developers can make use of several built-in functions and modules. While user-built functions are great for solving complex problems, they are difficult to implement and sometimes unnecessary because built-in functions can do the job.

1. print()

It is the most commonly used built-in function in Python. Everyone, from beginners to experienced programmers, uses the print() statement to display output on the computer screen. As previously stated, the content you want to display on the screen should be placed between the quotes.

2. abs()

It is a built-in function that returns the absolute value of any integer. If a negative integer is given as input, this function will return the positive value.

Program Code:

```
z = -65
print(abs(z))
```

Output:

```
65
```

3. round ()

It is a built-in mathematical function that returns the closest integer number to any given floating-point number.

Program Code:

```
x = 12.32
y = 4.23
print(round(x))
print(round(y))
```

Output:

```
12
4
```

4. max()

This built-in Python function returns the highest number among a set of numbers. This function can be applied to any data type, including lists and variables.

Program Code:

```
x = 31
y = 78
z = 36
mymax = max(x,y,z)
print(mymax)
```

Output:

```
78
```

5. min()

This built-in function returns the smallest number among a set of numbers.

Program Code:
```
x = 31
y = 78
z = 36
mymin = min(x,y,z)
print(mymin)
```
Output:
```
31
```

6. sorted()

It sorts all the elements in a list in either ascending or descending order, depending on your preference.

Program Code:
```
t = (5,857,165,43,430,60,753,15)
s = sorted(t)
print(s)
```
Output:
```
[5, 15, 43, 60, 165, 430, 753, 857]
```

7. sum()

sum() is a built-in function that takes as input a list or a tuple and adds their elements. All the elements of the list or tuple must have the same numerical data type. For example, if string data types are in the input, the program will fail with a type error.

Program Code:
```
t = (5,857,165,43,430,60,753,15)
s = sum(t)
print(s)
```
Output:
```
2328
```

8. len()

This built-in function returns the number of elements of the object in input.

Program Code:
```
t = (5,857,165,43,430,60,753,15)
s = len(t)
print(s)
```
Output:
```
8
```

9. type()

This function returns the data type of the object in input. If it is a function, the details about the parameters and arguments will be displayed as well.

Program Code:
```
t = 45.789
print(type(t))
```
Output:
```
<class 'float'>
```

String Functions

Strings are data types that require more attention from the programmer than other data types. Dozens of built-in functions in the Python core library have been created for programmers to make the most of data stored using strings.

1. strip()

It deletes the arguments passed to it as a parameter. The arguments will be removed from all instances where they appear.

Program Code:
```
text = "Python"
print(text.strip('hon'))
```
Output:
```
Pyt
```

2. replace()

It replaces one part of a string with another. If there are multiple words in the same string data type, you can specify how many to replace as a parameter.

Program Code:
```
text = "Have a great day!"
print(text.replace('great', 'wonderful'))
```
Output:
```
Have a wonderful day!
```

3. split()

It splits a string when the arguments you provided appear in the input text for the first time.

Program Code:
```
text = "There are three apples in the fridge"
print(text.split(' '))
```
Output:
```
['There', 'are', 'three', 'apples', 'in', 'the', 'fridge']
```
Since the argument we provided is a white space, in this case the output is a list with the words of the original string as elements.

4. join()

With this function you can insert a separator between the elements of a list, as long as they are characters.

Program Code:
```
country = ['Italy','France','Spain']
x = " ~ "
x = x.join(country)
print(x)
```
Output:
```
Italy ~ France ~ Spain
```

Exercises

1. Create a function that takes two numbers as parameters and returns the result of the sum of both numbers.

2. Create a function that takes a string as a parameter and returns the number of vowels in the string.

3. Create a function that takes two strings as parameters and returns a message indicating if both strings are equal or not.

4. Create a function that takes a number as a parameter and returns a message indicating if the number is positive, negative or zero.

5. Create a module with a function that takes a list as a parameter and returns the sum of all elements in the list. Import this module into another script and use the function to sum a list of numbers.

Chapter 9: Object Oriented Programming (OOP)

Until now we have discussed functional-oriented programming and provided several examples of code. While the functional programming paradigm is popular among independent developers, it can be difficult to implement when working with a team where many members must effectively communicate using their code.

Even though functional-oriented programming reduces a lot of code clutter, it is still difficult to import modules every time you create a new file. Importing more modules increases the program's run time exponentially.

Because of these issues, many programmers preferred to use Object-Oriented Programming languages such as Java during Python's initial release. But when Python 2 was released, everyone was enthusiastic to learn that Python had begun to support Object-Oriented Programming, transforming it into a multi-paradigm language.

With several examples, this chapter delves deeply into various object-oriented principles.

What Is OOP?

OOP is a popular programming paradigm in which classes and objects are used to organize functions into logical templates.

A class is a collection of data or methods that can be easily accessed using dot notation. Classes are accessible to variables and methods outside the class due to object behavior.

A Real-World Example:

Assume you are developing an application that explains details about various vehicles and models of those vehicles.

A functional programmer would create a function for each vehicle and then another for each model. It may appear simple when there are only a few vehicle models, but as the number of vehicle models grows, code reuse becomes difficult for developers.

In Object Oriented programming, however, the programmer will first create a 'vehicle' class and define various properties and values. The developer will then create a separate class for each type of vehicle. Because of the Object Oriented programming paradigm, the developer can access and call all those properties with a simple dot notation rather than creating functions for each property again.

Object Oriented programming saves time and is useful to reuse code thanks to features like polymorphism and inheritance.

How Do I Create Classes?

Classes are a way to create custom data types and they represent a blueprint from which objects are typically created. Classes include various logical entities such as attributes and methods. Specific rules must be followed when creating classes.

- All classes that are created must be preceded by the keyword 'class.'
- Variables created within a class are nothing more than class attributes.
- All attributes in a class are public and can be used at any time by using the . (dot) operator.

The syntax for class creation:

```
class ClassName:
        # Class-level attributes
        Definition of the attributes

        # Initialization method
        The self method that we'll discuss

        # Class methods
        Specific methods (functions) of the class
```

In Python, you can't use reserved keywords for class names. Otherwise, a traceback error will occur, causing the application to crash.

How Do I Create Objects?

In Python programming, an object is an entity that has a state and behavior. Everything within a class can be considered an object. A variable created within a class, for example, can be used as an object. Objects are frequently used by programmers who are unaware of their existence.

What exactly is an object?

- Every object is made up of a state. A state usually reflects the properties of an object.
- Every object has a behavior. The behavior of an object changes depending on the method in which it is used.
- All objects have an identity. Objects use identity to interact with one another.

Assume there is a cat class that describes different cat features and behavior. Objects in that class can be of various types.

- The name of the cat is typically used to identify the object
- Attributes such as cat age, type, and color can be used to describe the state of an object.
- Behaviors of an object include jumping, sleeping, and running in relation to a cat.

How to create an object?

All you have to do to create an object is give it a name. For instance, if the 'Cat' class is defined, we can write:

Program Code:

```
obj = Cat()
```

This will generate an object called 'obj' belonging to the Cat class.

The Self Method

You should be aware of the self method, which is automatically created when a class is created.

The concept of a self method is very similar to that of pointers in other programming languages such as C and C++.

If you want to call the methods, you must provide at least one argument to the self method. Every method that an object invokes is automatically transformed to a self object.

The __init__ Method

The __init__ method is similar to C++ and Java constructors. When a class is started, it runs as a default method. As a result, if you want to create an object with an initial value, you must enter those values into the __init method as a developer.

We'll make an example now by using self and the ___init__ method.

Program Code:

```
# Define a class called "Person" with the "name" attribute
class Person:
    # Define a class attribute shared by all instances of the class
    species = "Homo sapiens"

    def __init__(self, name):
        # Initialize the name attribute as an instance attribute
        self.name = name

# Create two instances of the Person class with different names
person1 = Person("Alex")
person2 = Person("Sam")

# Print the names of each person
print("Name of person 1:", person1.name)
print("Name of person 2:", person2.name)
# Print the species attribute shared by all instances of the class
print("Species:", Person. species)
print(person1.name,'and',person2.name,'are',Person.species)
```

Output:

```
Name of person 1: Alex
Name of person 2: Sam
Species: Homo sapiens
Alex and Sam are Homo sapiens
```

In the previous example, we defined a class as well as instance attributes. There are a few simple rules to keep in mind:

- You must provide a class name
- You must create at least one attribute
- You must provide a self argument and a __init__ method
- An object must be instantiated
- Following object instantiation, you can create instance attributes that can use the object.

Classes and Objects With Methods

In the previous example, a class attribute is created, followed by a method and the __init__ function. Finally, two objects are instantiated, and they are accessed using dot notation.

Program Code:

```python
class Person:
    species = "Homo sapiens"

    def __init__(self, name):
        self.name = name

    # Define a method to say hello
    def say_hello(self):
        return "Hello, my name is " + self.name

person1 = Person("Alex")
person2 = Person("Sam")

# Print the names of each person
print("Name of person 1:", person1.name)
print("Name of person 2:", person2.name)

# Call the say_hello method on each person
print(person1.say_hello())
print(person2.say_hello())
```

Output:

```
Name of person 1: Alex
Name of person 2: Sam
Hello, my name is Alex
Hello, my name is Sam
```

Explanation:

In the above example, a class attribute is created, and then a method is created along with the __init__ function. In the end, the object is instantiated, and the object is accessed by using the dot notation.

Inheritance

One of the most important aspects of Object-Oriented programming is inheritance. Inheritance refers to the process of defining a new class without adding new methods or arguments, but rather deriving them from other classes. The new class is commonly referred to as the child class. The parent class is the class from which all methods are inherited.

Real-World Example:

When developing real-world applications, inheritance comes in handy in a variety of situations. Assume you are developing a camera mobile application for iOS.

While creating the application, you may need to create several modules for the various functions it provides. You've noticed that you're reusing code for GUI interfaces after a few months of development because your team is still using function-oriented programming.

You decided to use an object-oriented framework for your project to save time and money. Since you're now using the OOP paradigm, you can reuse the code you've already written for GUI interfaces and link it to the new classes you're creating. This saves time and energy by allowing programmers to add new features without having to rewrite the old ones.

Syntax for Python inheritance:

```
class BaseClass:
        { Body of base class }
class DerivedClass(Baseclass):
        { Body of derived class }
```

Please keep in mind that both base and derived classes must follow all the previously described class rules.

Program Code:

```python
# Define a base class "Polygon" with a method to return the number of
        edges
class Polygon:
    def __init__(self, num_edges):
        self.num_edges = num_edges


    def edges(self):
        return self.num_edges


# Define a subclass "Rectangle" based on the Polygon class
class Rectangle(Polygon):
    def __init__(self, length, width):
        # Call the __init__ method of the parent class to initialize
        the number of edges
        Polygon.__init__(self, 4)
        self.length = length
        self.width = width


    # Define a method to calculate the area of the rectangle
    def area(self):
        return self.length * self.width


# Create an instance of the Rectangle class
rect = Rectangle(40, 10)


# Print the number of edges and the area of the rectangle
print("Number of edges:", rect.edges())
print("Area:", rect.area())
```

Output:

```
Number of edges: 4
Area: 50
```

Explanation:

In the previous example, we defined the class 'Polygon' first, and then built the second class 'Rectangle' on top of it. A rectangle with dimensions of 40 by 10 is created. When the 'area' method is called, the area of the square is computed. You can create another polygon class in the future by simply writing a method to calculate the area.

With enough knowledge of Object-Oriented Programming, you can create classes and objects that can interact in order to create software that uses many components and performs multiple tasks. Look at the open-source code hosted on GitHub to learn more about OOP.

Exercises

1. Create a class called Person with a constructor that takes in the person's name, age, and occupation. The class should have methods get_name(), get_age(), and get_occupation() that return the respective values. Create an instance of the class and call the methods to display the values.

2. Create a class called Student that inherits from Person. The class must have a constructor that takes in the name, age, occupation, and a list of subjects. The class should have a method get_subjects() that returns the list of subjects. Create an instance of the class and call the methods to display the values.

3. Create a class called Rectangle with a constructor that takes in the width and height. The class should have methods get_area() and get_perimeter() that return the area and perimeter of the rectangle, respectively. Create an instance of the class and call the methods to display the values.

4. Create a class called BankAccount with a constructor that takes in the owner's name, balance, and type of account. The class should have methods get_balance(), deposit(amount), and withdraw(amount) that return the balance, deposit an amount, and withdraw an amount respectively. Create an instance of the class and call the methods to display the values.

5. Create a class called Vehicle with a constructor that takes in the make, model, and year. The class should have methods get_make(), get_model(), and get_year() that return the respective values. Create two classes, Car and Truck, that inherit from Vehicle. The Car class should have an additional method get_type() that returns "Car" and the Truck class should have an additional method get_type() that returns "Truck". Create instances of both classes and call the methods to display the values.

Chapter 10: Files in Python

Python stores data in variables for both static and dynamic data. While variables are ideal for storing data during the execution of a program, they can be difficult to use when the data is sensitive and needs to be reused repeatedly. Variables can self-destruct in order to clear memory, which is inconvenient for users who want to save or reuse their data for multiple purposes. Python provides files to better interact with data of any size or format. Understanding file operations and implementing them in your programs is essential for creating better software as a Python programmer.

File Paths

Python programmers typically work with multiple files and two parameters. The first is the file name, which makes it easy to find, the second is the file path.

For example, if file.pdf is the name of a file, then "C:/ users/ downloads/file.pdf" is the path format of a file. The file extension in the file name 'file.pdf' is pdf. To manage files, most operating systems employ an efficient file management system.

It is critical to understand file management techniques. For this reason, you must understand the fundamentals of file managers used in the operating systems you are working in. For example, Windows use file explorer to manage files, whereas Mac systems use Finder. Regardless of the operating system and file manager you use, files are typically organized in a logical hierarchical order using root directories, folders, and subdirectories.

Hierarchical Arrangement of Files

For the program to detect the file location, you must enter the entire path. The entire path of the file is generally written hierarchically in order to determine the directory, subdirectories, and folders.

For example, in 'C:/users/sample/example.pdf,' C is the system's root directory, and sample and users are subdirectories within it. Because there may be multiple files with the same name in different folders, it is critical to use the entire path to determine the file's location.

As a programmer, you should be aware that Windows systems use Backslashes to differentiate between the root directory and subdirectories. Other operating systems, such as Mac and Linux, use forward slashes to distinguish between root and subdirectories.

If you don't want to use back or forward slashes while entering code on the terminal for whatever reason, you can use a function called os.path.join.

Program Code:
```
os.path.join('C', 'first', 'second')
```
Output:
```
'C\first\second'
```

Current Working Directory

While running complex code, you may need to interact with multiple files in the same directory as a Python programmer. A function called os.getcwd() can be used to help programmers interact with other files in the same directory. When your absolute path is identified, all files in the directory or subdirectory will be shown as output.

Creating New Folders

Several Python programs usually require users to generate files or the application to create files in different directories on its own. A save file for a game, for example, may be generated automatically by the software without any user intervention. All Python programmers must be aware of the importance of creating new folders for the applications they create. To create a new directory, use the os.makedirs() function.

Program Code:
```
import os
os.makedirs('D: /user/ Python/myfolder')
```
In the previous example, we first imported the 'os' module containing the system function design. The makedirs() function was then called with a path as the function parameter. "myfolder" is the name of the new folder created in the directory by the above function. You can check by opening your file manager or typing cd into a command prompt.

Please make sure to provide an absolute path to the directory where you want to create a new folder.

Functions to Manage Files

Files are complex and require a plethora of built-in functions to function properly. You can easily manipulate, open, and close files with Python from your IDE or terminal. By default, the Python interpreter can run both .txt and.py extension files.

If you want to work with file types like pdf and jpg, you'll need to install third-party libraries. By experienced Python programmers, these file types are referred to as binary file types.

To begin, we will create a file called example.txt on the path "D: /user/Python/example.txt" to help you understand the concepts of Files. You are free to use your path when creating a file.

This example txt file will be used to describe file functions such as open(), close(), write(), and read().

Assume the example.txt file contains the following:

Content:
```
This is a Python file.
```

How to Open Files

It is quite simple to open files with a Python command. All you need to know is the file's absolute path and how to use the open() function.

Program Code:
```
myfile = open ('D: /user / Python / example.txt ')
# This will open the file
```

The open() function, along with the parameter, is used in the example. The parameter in this example is the path provided to open a file. When a file is opened, the Python interpreter cannot read or write it, but the user can read it using the default viewer in which it was opened.

Before running this statement, make sure you have the necessary software to open the files. For example, if you try to open an.mp4 video file and there is not a native application that can open it, it will not be a viable solution.

What Happens?

When the interpreter locates the open() function, a new file object is created, and all changes made during this phase must be saved in order to be reflected in the original file. If the file is not saved, the Python interpreter will ignore all changes.

How to Read Files

When Python opens a file with the open() function, it creates a new object, and the Python interpreter can now easily read the entire file's content with the read() function.

Program Code:
```
filecontent = myfile.read()
# read() will scan all the content present in the file
```

Output:
```
This is a Python file.
```

In the previous example, we used the read() function to send the scanned data from the file to a new variable called 'filecontent'. Depending on the complexity of the file, you can also send the information into files to lists, tuples, or dictionaries.

While the read() function just prints the file content, the readlines() function can be used to organise the content of a file to new lines.

We will use a simple example to demonstrate this Python feature. First, in your working directory, create a new file called 'mynewfile.txt.' After opening the file, enter a few lines, as shown below.

mynewfile.txt:

```
This is an example of a document
We are simply connecting the dots
This information will be used to manipulate text
The Python interpreter is fast
```

Let's now call the readlines() function on the terminal.

Program Code:

```
myfile = open(mynewfile.txt)
# This variable helps us open a new file with the name provided
myfile.readlines()
```

Output:

```
['This is an example of a document \n', ' We are simply connecting the
dots \n', ' This information will be used to manipulate text  \n',
'Python interpreter is fast']
```

The output included a newline character \n for each line in the file. There are numerous advanced file functions that can be used when developing real-world applications.

How to Write Content to Files

You can use the write() function to insert new data into any file. The write() function is very similar to the print() function, which is used by programmers to display content on the screen. It displays the contents of the file with the name you specify.

The open() function allows programmers to open the file in write mode. All you need to do is append an argument to let the interpreter know you want to open the file and add your own content.

Once you've finished writing into the file, use the close() method to close it and save it in its default location.

Program Code:

```
myfile = open('example.txt', 'w')
#This makes the file open in write mode
myfile.write ('This is how we write on files! \n')
myfile.close()
```

The output will show the content of the screen as well as the number of characters. You can also append text as an argument by using 'a'.

Example:

```
myfile = open('example.txt', 'a')
# The file is open in write mode
example.write('This is a new version')
# The above statement will be added to the file provided
myfile.close()
```

To check whether the message has been appended, use the read function, as shown below.

```
myfile = read(example.txt)
print(myfile)
```

You can usually copy, paste, or cut files and folders using the default file manager functions, such as Windows Explorer and Mac finder. However, in Python you must use a built-in library known as shutil, It creates programming components that can be used to quickly copy, move, or delete files.

To use the shutil library's default functions, you must first import the library.

Chapter 11: Exception Handling

All applications occasionally crash as a result of incorrect user input or an error that occurs. It is possible to inform the user about why the application has crashed. If you can't help them, your software should at the very least detect that the application has collapsed and send the logs to your server to help them find solutions. Giving users a heads-up about errors is the bare minimum that modern application developers can do to improve their user experience.

Exception handling is a computer programming feature that helps developers to write scenarios for which an application may crash and explicitly instruct the user if this occurs.

Do you remember the famous "This application has stopped responding" with a red 'x' mark on Windows systems? It is one of the most well-known exception handling interfaces in any system. While your exceptions do not have to be of the highest quality, they should be adequate for a better end-user experience.

In Python development, writing valid exceptions is considered a sophisticated skill. Exception handling also assists programmers in detecting bugs and logical defects in a program early in the workflow. An exception also saves a significant amount of time during testing and maintenance.

Exception Handling Example:
- Go to your profile and try to tweet an image that is larger than 24MB. After loading, the Twitter web or app interface will display a popup informing you that your image cannot be uploaded due to its larger size.
- In this case, Twitter developers have built an exception handling interface to help users understand why their images are not being uploaded. Exception handling is an excellent tool for improving the user experience.
- All well-known third-party libraries include exception handling methods that you can import and use in your applications.

We will teach you how to handle exceptions using the Divide-by-zero error.

When you divide a number by zero, the value is usually undefined because it is referred to as an infinite value. Similarly, if a user of your application attempts to divide a number by zero, you must display a ZeroDivisionError. This error can be displayed using try and except statements.

'Try' and 'Except'

When creating exception handling tasks, you should be aware of the leading programming components try and except. The try block is where developers must specify the likelihood of finding the error in the Python interpreter. The except block, on the other hand, requires information about what to do if a specific error that we defined occurs during program execution.

Program Code:

```
# Try and except block in a function
def divide32(x):
    try:
        A = 32/x
        print(A)
    except ZeroDivisionError:
        print ("I can't divide by 0")


divide32(8)
divide32(0)
divide32(16)
```

Output:

```
4.0
I can't divide by 0
2.0
```

We started with a try and except block that told the interpreter where we could expect an error popup and what information should be displayed if there was one.

Different Types of Errors

Python documentation contains a plethora of system errors. When we discussed the Zero division error in the previous example, you may have noticed a straightforward approach. Different errors have different methods for avoiding them or running applications even when they are present.

Understanding the causes of some system errors can help you understand the fundamentals of debugging your applications.

Value errors

These errors occur when you pass arguments to a function that are not of the type that they accept. A value error can cause your application to crash unexpectedly.

Uploading a pdf file when only image files are permitted is an example of an exception trigger.

Import error

These errors occur when you are unable to import a module directly into your program. They are typically caused by a network connection failure or issues with online package managers.

Example of an Exception Trigger: You are unable to sync your data on your private cloud accounts due to an import error.

OS error

You may occasionally encounter issues because the software is incompatible with your operating system version. These errors frequently occur because the system kernel does not understand what the application is saying. These errors are fairly common when using Linux distributions.

Example of an Exception Trigger: The application crashes because the host is running an unsupported version of an operating system.

Type error

This error typically occurs when a user or developer enters a value for a data type that the application does not yet support.

Name error

When a variable or function that has not yet been defined in the program is called, this error occurs.

Index error

Index errors typically occur when you provide an index that is greater than the list you have created.

Chapter 12: Advanced Programming

Many third-party Python frameworks provide specific functionalities to programmers. It's sufficient to import the base libraries. That's why Python's popularity has skyrocketed. Libraries are great for developers to create real-world applications that ordinary users can use. You should be aware of certain commonly used Python libraries to write valid complex code without having to start from scratch.

The source codes for the majority of these libraries will be available for exploration on websites such as GitHub or Bitbucket.

Pip Package Manager

All operating systems make applications available to their users. Python isn't an operating system, but rather a software interpreter. Any software that is not written in Python can't run using a Python interpreter because the Python interpreter does not understand the source code used by that software.

There are thousands of paid and free Python software downloads available from many sources. A simple Google search for Python software for the domain you are interested in can provide thousands of results. To install this software on your own, you will need at least a basic understanding of executable files.

Python offers package managers to download package files into your operating system to be immediately executed. In this way, you can easily install the software you need. While there are many third-party Python package managers, the default pip is the most common and every Python programmer should be familiar with.

Why Using Pip

- New packages and dependencies can be installed.
- There is an index that lists all Python package repositories that are available on pip servers.
- Before installing the software, use it to go over the requirements.
- Remove all packages and dependencies that you no longer use.

First, check if pip is installed on your system. Pip is usually included with the Python.

Terminal Code:
```
$ pip —version
```
If it prints out the pip version information details, your system has the package manager installed. If not, you may need to manually download and install it from the official website.

How to Install Packages?

To install packages, you should always use the syntax format shown below.

$ pip install name_of_the_software

For example, if you want to install the "Seaborn" package, the syntax is the following:

```
$ pip install seaborn
```

To check the information associated with the content before installing, use the command below:

```
$ pip show seaborn
```

This terminal code will return a lot of metadata information, including the Author, Package name and location.

Use the code syntax format below to uninstall any package installed on your system using the pip package manager.

Syntax:

$ pip uninstall nameofthepackage

For example, to uninstall the Seaborn package you previously installed, use the command below:

```
$ pip uninstall seaborn
```

You can also search for a package using the code format shown below.

$ pip search name_of_the_package

This will show you all packages from the package index for you to examine and select from.

Virtual Environment

Typically, when you install a package, you are also installing a number of dependencies. These dependencies may occasionally overlap with other software, causing the package to fail to install. To help developers in creating independent projects, the 'virtualenv' package can be used to create an isolated virtual environment.

First, use the pip package manager to install the 'virtualenv' package.

Installation command:

```
$ pip install virtualenv
```

Once the package is installed, you can use the below command to create a new directory using a virtual machine.

```
$ virtualenv mydir
```

All the packages, files, and software you install will be saved in this new directory, without interfering with any system dependencies or packages. To begin, run the following command to activate the virtual machine.

Terminal Command:

```
$ source mydir/bin/activate
```

After you've installed all of your packages, deactivate this virtual environment with the following command:

Terminal Command:
```
(mydir) $ deactivate
```

The sys Module

To master Python it's crucial to understand how a Python interpreter works. An interpreter typically parses every variable, method or literal in the code before executing a logically written program and checking for syntax, type, and index errors. It is important to examine how an interpreter works and stores information required for the use of specific software.

The Sys module in Python makes it simple for developers to check this information.
```
import sys
```

path

This sys library argument will tell you the default path of the Python interpreter installed on your system:
```
print(sys.path)
```

argv

This method will return a list of all the existing modules in the system:
```
print(sys.argv)
```

copyright

This method will show the user the copyright information for the Python interpreter or software:
```
print(sys.copyright)
```

getrefcount

This method shows how frequently a program uses a variable or object:
```
print(sys.getrefcount(myvariable))
```

Unit Testing

Before developing, a programmer must ensure that the program follows all Python's guidelines. Even if the logic in your programs is correct, it may cause problems in the future due to practical issues. These bottleneck situations should be avoided in order to provide a better user experience.

Python allows and encourages programmers to check their code using unit testing frameworks. The framework 'unittest' is installed by default to force programmers to create testing conditions from scratch for their programs.

How Do Unit Tests Work?

You may become overwhelmed when testing their code because the Python documentation does not provide a specific set of rules for conducting unit tests. However, experienced programmers always emphasize that it is best to start testing code for methods first and then expand to other programming components.

- Using this methodology, you can test any part of the software.
- The tested code can be easily shared with other developers. Furthermore, eventual build and runtime errors during this process will be shared with your team.
- You can group tests and call them collections, and then manually organize them to keep these tests up to date.

Other third-party frameworks can be installed by programmers to improve their unit testing skills.

Scrapy

Scrapy is a Python library designed specifically for scraping purposes. Spiders are typically used to scrape data from dynamic websites and search engines. Scrapy is great to create advanced spiders capable of intuitively extracting data from web or mobile pages.

To install Scrapy, enter the following code into any package manager.

Installation command:

```
pip install scrapy
```

Requests

Requests is a Python library used to create HTTP requests for web or mobile applications. You can easily manage requests and responses for all web content that your application uses with Requests.

The web response data is typically in JSON format. t is normally difficult to read, but Requests parses the JSON file and displays the information in a readable manner. Scrappers also make use of the requests library to build automation software for major websites.

Use the default pip package to install Requests.

Installation command:

```
pip install requests
```

Pygame

Python is also used to create games for handheld consoles and mobile devices. Pygame is a popular third-party gaming framework among independent developers worldwide. Pygame includes both multimedia and physics libraries, allowing developers to create 2D and 3D games. Pygame also includes sound, mouse, keyboard, and accelerometer components for creating highly interactive games.

Most Pygame developers create games for Android phones and tablets because the SDL Pygame framework is highly adaptable to these devices.

Use the following command to install Pygame on your local system.

Installation command:

```
pip install pygame
```

Beautiful Soup

Beautiful Soup is a popular Python scraping library that can retrieve HTML and XML data from a variety of sources with a single click. It can generate an efficient parse tree of the various directories and sub-directories present on the website, allowing users to easily organize the scraped information.

Before scraping, Beautiful Soup understands the most recent technologies, such as HTML 5 elements on a web page. Beautiful Soup is used by several third-party software, including Ahrefs, to handle their premium keyword research tools, which frequently need to scrape data from billions of pages on the internet.

Use pip to install Beautiful Soup on your local system.

Installation command:

```
pip install beautifulsoup
```

Pillow

Pillow is one of many Python libraries that make image manipulation simple. Image enhancement is required in a variety of computer domains, and Pillow makes it possible by leveraging the legacy PIL project, which was considered a better image manipulation library written in C.

Pillow is a fork of the PIL project, which is no longer being developed. Pillow supports a variety of image formats, including png, jpeg, gif and ttf. Furthermore, you can use Pillow's built-in methods to perform many photo editing functions, like rotating, resizing, cropping, and changing filters.

Use pip to install the Pillow library on your local system.

Installation command:

```
pip install pillow
```

Tensorflow

Tensorflow is a well-known Machine Learning library for building advanced neural networks. Many developers also use Tensorflow within Deep Learning frameworks to develop software components that are frequently embedded in Deep Learning applications like facial recognition. Google created Tensorflow to make the development of complex machine learning models easier. However, it was later made open source so that enthusiastic developers could contribute to the project.

Tensorflow can be installed using any package manager, such as pip.

Installation command:

```
pip install tensorflow
```

Scikit learn

Scikit learn is a widely used machine learning model creation tool that is similar to TensorFlow. Many developers use it to create data analysis and analytics software. Scikit learn makes it simple for developers to incorporate advanced machine learning models into their code, such as clustering, Random forests, and K-means algorithms. Scikit learn also supports complex neural networking algorithms used in scientific research, such as the development of genetic algorithms. To install it use the following command.

Installation command:

```
pip install sci-kit learn
```

Pandas

Data analysts are in love with Pandas because it is one of the most popular third-party libraries. While R is more popular among data analysts than Python, Pandas is still a good library for developers who want to create advanced data-analysis models. Pandas makes it simple to import and export huge amounts of data in a variety of formats, including SQL, JSON, and Excel. Furthermore, you can use Pandas with greater precision than other libraries for data cleaning and arrangement, which are high-level data analysis techniques.

Use package managers such as pip to install Pandas on your local system.

Installation command:

```
pip install pandas
```

Matplotlib

Matplotlib is a well-known Python library that is used in conjunction with Scipy to implement high-level mathematical functions in your code. Scipy and Matplotlib can be used together to create multidimensional arrays, which can then be used to write complex code to solve real-world scientific challenges. Many computer scientists rely on these libraries to keep their workflows running smoothly.

Matplotlib displays all acquired data in beautiful graphs to help you better understand the data flow. Tkinter is also used to logically arrange data. While Scipy focuses on scientific and technical computing, Matplotlib focuses on data visualization for enthusiasts and organizations.

Use pip to install Matplotlib on your local system.

Installation command:

```
pip install matplotlib
```

To use some of Matplotlib's advanced functions, make sure Scipy is installed using the command below.

Installation command:

```
pip install scipy
```

Twisted

Developers of web-based Python applications must be familiar with various networking concepts. While the core Python library provides enough resources and methods to write efficient networking code, it is always recommended that you use libraries such as Twisted to create complex code more easily. With a single click, Twisted implements networking protocols such as UDP, TCP, and HTTP. Twisted is the default networking component library for many websites, including Twitch.

Use pip to install Twisted.

Installation command:

```
pip install twisted
```

GitHub for Programmers

GitHub is useful for programmers because it allows them to collaborate with teams remotely. GitHub is based on a peer-to-peer GIT repository, so the changes of your code will be reflected in your teammates' computers as soon as they are connected to the internet.

GitHub provides two versions: free and professional. When you use the free version, your code is accessible to anyone who has a GitHub account. With the pro version, your code will be private, and only members of your team will be able to access it. Furthermore, all private repositories use advanced encryption algorithms to safeguard your data.

Why Is GitHub Essential for Python Programmers?

Regardless of the computer domain you work in, you may need to use third-party frameworks and libraries available on GitHub when creating projects. You can use GitHub or one of several third-party clients to instantly interact with local repositories. Dependencies are used by GitHub and all Git-supported clients to easily sync libraries and modules into your code. The Git server's 'commit' option allows you to make changes to the code.

Use the Python shell to run the following command to create a new repository in your GIT server.

Installation command:

```
$ git config —global root "my project."
```

When you enter the git code into the console, a new project is created, and you can now create folders for your project. To start creating a directory on the root of your project, run the command below.

```
$ mkdir. ("Name of the repository: ")
```
If you don't know anything about the GIT server or project you're working on, type the following command into your console.
```
$ git status
```
In this way you are ready to begin developing your open-source project to help other programmers in your domain.

Conclusion

First and foremost, congratulations on finishing a comprehensive Python guide. This book has covered a variety of in-depth Python topics that will help you in writing high-quality code for your projects. However, consistent practice with the fundamentals taught in this book is required to improve. Working on projects or practicing competitive coding will only increase your expertise.

Some features of experienced programmers have contributed to their success in their passionate journey with computers and technology. They usually develop several habits that help them become better programmers. As a beginner, it is critical that you understand some of these characteristics and incorporate them into your workflow to increase performance within a topic or a group of topics.

Programmer Features

Foundations first

You must understand the fundamentals as much as possible. Writing code for difficult tasks with a solid foundation becomes much easier over time. To strengthen your foundations, familiarize yourself with the Python style guide, which strives for simplicity. Writing simple code and following the Zen of Python rules will help in the improvement of your fundamental knowledge.

Break problems into smaller parts

As a programmer, you must solve complex and complicated problems. Not all problems can be solved with a single logical step. To solve a problem with better runtime execution, a programmer must break it down into smaller problems. This philosophy can assist programmers in developing software with fewer bugs that requires a minimal unit testing strategy.

Find your specialty

It is impossible for any programmer to be proficient in every computer domain. You should have clear what computer domain you are most interested in as a programmer. Experiment with various computing systems to better understand what computer domain you like. Python, for example, is versatile and can be a great resource for data scientists, web developers, or systems engineers. Don't force yourself to learn a little bit of everything; instead, focus on mastering a single domain.

You will actually learn from errors

Errors can be demotivating, especially if you're just starting out. Anytime you get an error, copy the traceback error and search for it in Google or ChatGPT. You will find several solutions to the problem, and fixing it on your own will help you better understand the fundamentals of Python.

Learn to implement algorithms

To improve your writing skills in terms of programming logic, you should learn sorting and search algorithms. Understanding mathematical concepts will also help in the intuitive approach to complex problems. While competitive programmers typically approach problems differently than software developers, understanding their approach can help you overcome various roadblocks that may arise during the software development process.

Python can be used to implement binary search algorithms, graph algorithms, and complex data structures such as Stacks and Queues. To approach Python from an algorithmic standpoint, we recommend using websites like LeetCode.

Get familiar with GitHub

One of the most important resources to be aware of is GitHub. All open-source code is generally available through git repositories. As a result, if you want to make any changes to these repositories, you must contact the repository owners using GitHub commands like 'push' and 'commit.' All companies looking for developers prefer people with GitHub experience because it allows them to quickly integrate you into their team.

Don't overwork

Even though this is not a technical tip, understanding the slow and steady philosophy employed by experienced developers is critical. Never try to take in too much information at once. **Consistency beats performance** and it is more important in the early stages of your career. As a result, instead of cramming the information in a few days, schedule a few hours of Python studying every day. Participate in programs like 100daysofPython on platforms such as Twitter to keep yourself motivated and consistent.

Be aware of testing procedures

Before developing software to end users, it must be thoroughly tested. Understanding unit testing workflows such as Alpha and beta testing will help you provide more functional software with fewer known bugs. Use a user-reporting strategy to recreate bugs more easily in your working machine and resolve them as soon as possible. Clearing bugs requires experience and, at times, an expert opinion. Don't be afraid to ask for help in forums.

Keep a healthy work-life balance

Regardless of your chosen profession, keeping a balance between work and personal life is important. To get the most out of your work time, especially as a programmer, you must be aware of tasks and time management. If you work as a freelancer, apps like Things and Session can help you manage your tasks effectively. Furthermore, using techniques like the Pomodoro technique can help you clear more bugs in less time.

What Next?

I'm glad you're along for the ride as we learn Python. Programming is enjoyable, and no matter how fast you learn, only practice will make you a great developer. So, using the knowledge you've gained from this book, start working on your projects.

If you're stumped as to what projects to try, here are some project ideas to get you started.

- Create a management system for a public library in your community.
- Create a suburban metro railway reservation system.
- Using the Django library, create a simple website.
- Use Pygame to create a classic Python game.
- Parse Twitter data to build a bot that automatically retweets popular tweets.

I hope that your personal growth journey is successful in every way!

Acknowledgments

Writing a technical book is never an easy task. It requires a lot of time, effort, and focus. This book on Python is no exception. The journey of writing this book has been full of challenges and struggles, but I am grateful for the experience.

I would like to express my deep gratitude to one of my professors, Mr. Albert Johnson. He has been a constant source of inspiration and guidance throughout my academic and professional life. His teachings on programming and Python have been invaluable to me and I have tried my best to incorporate his wisdom and insights in this book.

I would also like to thank my coworker Alex very much. He's been very encouraging to me as I've worked on this project. He has shared his expertise, provided constructive feedback and encouraged me to push through the difficult moments.

I owe the greatest debt of gratitude to my wife Kate, who has always been there for me and pushed me forward. She has been my number one cheerleader and has never wavered in her faith in me, even when I questioned my own abilities. Her love, understanding and patience have sustained me through the long nights of writing and editing.

I also want to take a moment to thank you, the reader, for taking the time to delve into the world of Python with me. Your support and interest in this book is what makes all of the hard work and struggles worth it.

As you embark on your journey to learn Python and become a skilled programmer, I want to encourage you to never give up. While the path to mastery may be exhausting, the benefits of succeeding are well worth the effort. Anything worth having is worth working hard for, and if you put in the time and effort, you can get it.

So, take a deep breath, embrace the challenge, and never stop learning. The possibilities are endless, and I have no doubt that you will succeed in your endeavors.

Thank you for joining me on this journey, and I hope you enjoy the book.

Philip

References

Parmar, N. (n.d.). Conditional statement in Python. Naukri Learning. https://www.naukri.com/learning/articles/conditional-statement-in-python/

O'Neil, C. (2021, June 7). How to install Python on Windows 10. DigitalOcean. https://www.digitalocean.com/community/tutorials/install-python-windows-10

McEwen, J. (2021, May 24). Coding: What is PyCharm? Emeritus. https://emeritus.org/blog/coding-what-is-pycharm/

O'Neil, C. (2020, December 9). The Python and operator explained. Real Python. https://realpython.com/python-and-operator/

LearnPython.org. (n.d.). Variables and types. Learn Python. https://www.learnpython.org/en/Variables_and_Types

VanderPlas, J. (2018, November 20). Understanding data types in Python. Python Data Science Handbook. https://jakevdp.github.io/PythonDataScienceHandbook/02.01-understanding-data-types.html

Wilder, R. (2015). Functions. In Writing Electronic Text: A Guide to Good Practice. https://rwet.decontextualize.com/book/functions/

Arras, L. (2021, June 2). Object-oriented programming in Python 3. Real Python. https://realpython.com/python3-object-oriented-programming/

★ A GIFT FOR YOU (DOWNLOAD IT) ★

SCAN THE QR CODE BELOW AND

- GET THE MOST COMMON PYTHON INTERVIEW QUESTIONS AND ANSWERS

- GET THE SOLUTIONS TO THE EXERCISES

Made in United States
North Haven, CT
30 March 2023

34754489R00063